Speaking of Success

COLLECTED WISDOM,
INSIGHTS AND REFLECTIONS

Speaking of Success

COLLECTED WISDOM, INSIGHTS AND REFLECTIONS

Pamela Wallin

KEY PORTER  BOOKS

National Library of Canada Cataloguing in Publication Data

Wallin, Pamela, 1953–
    Speaking of success: collected wisdom, insights and reflections

ISBN 1-55263-370-5

1. Celebrities—Biography. 2. Biography—20th century. 3. Success. I. Title.

CT120.W34 2001   920'.009'045   C2001-901679-4

THE CANADA COUNCIL | LE CONSEIL DES ARTS
FOR THE ARTS | DU CANADA
SINCE 1957 | DEPUIS 1957

ONTARIO ARTS COUNCIL
CONSEIL DES ARTS DE L'ONTARIO

The publisher gratefully acknowledges the support of the Canada Council for the Arts and the Ontario Arts Council for its publishing program.

We acknowledge the financial support of the Government of Canada through the Book Publishing Industry Development Program (BPIDP) for our publishing activities.

Key Porter Books Limited
70 The Esplanade
Toronto, Ontario
Canada M5E 1R2

www.keyporter.com

Cover Design: Peter Maher
Text Design: Jack Steiner
Electronic formatting: Heidy Lawrance Associates

Printed and bound in Canada

01 02 03 04 05 06 6 5 4 3 2

Contents

Acknowledgements

Time and space are precious commodities in the world of books, and, as you can imagine, the material in this one often defied easy categorization—an insight in one area was often just as relevant in another. So, the true meaning of this book will be in the eye of the beholder. Each of you will read a slightly different book and you will all take away something unique, as I'm sure you do when you watch my conversations on television. Let me thank all of you, either as readers or as viewers over the years, for your part in the work we do. The honesty in your letters and e-mails and in the comments you've shared in person have made my work—including this endeavour—worthwhile.

I also want to offer my gratitude to the many "guests" who have so willingly shared their ideas and their valuable time and whose wise words are the heart of and reason for this collection. Friend or stranger, your thoughts have inspired, amused, soothed and saddened. But, most importantly, they've made me think. Thank you for sharing what you know.

While sorting and selecting and poring over hundreds of hours of tapes and transcripts was a gruelling task, it was also wonderful because it was a chance to meet all these remarkable people again. Enter Shelley Ambrose, one of the great wonders of the world. Her relentless and tireless commitment to this project meant endless hours of watching interviews and transcribing exchanges—not to mention suffering through an inordinate number of my hairstyles, some of which, she says, were quite ghastly. She risked her eyesight, but never lost her vision or optimism about the importance of this project. Her judgements are astute. She is a woman of extraordinary talent and patience. And, although you'll not find her words quoted in this volume, her heart and hand grace every page. I consider myself truly blessed that you are both a friend and a colleague.

In the early stages of this process, Edna Barker gently chided me into understanding that less is more. Many thanks for your pithy and pointed comments and for your attention to detail. And my thanks as well to all the wonderful folks at Frontier College who offered support and technology and, on one occasion, a place to work when the power went out and rendered my computer screen blank.

Susan Folkins, my editor at Key Porter, may regret that she volunteered for this project, but she was invaluable in making this book of collected wisdom wiser. She helped us wrestle the never-ending supply of material into a meaningful manuscript. Her sharp instinct and calm, quiet demeanour were an antidote to the inevitable sense of crisis that emerges whenever deadlines come into play. I am truly grateful for your kindness and your talent.

Publisher Anna Porter believed in this project and never gave up on it or me. She and Julian offered much-needed care and feeding along the way, both figuratively and literally. Thank you for being such good friends. And to all the people who make up the extended Key Porter family and who embraced this project and set about trying to make it happen—everything from cover design to book tour—I am indebted for your willing efforts.

This book would not have been possible without Beverley Bowen, who minds the store and keeps my life on track through this and many other endeavours. And while the list is too long, my profound thanks to all the producers and researchers who, over the years, and at all hours of the night and day, have brought these great minds to the table and allowed me to feast. Your support and shared passion have given me the best years of my life. And to Michael, for the words of encouragement and for the wonderful adventure when I had reached the end of my tether, much love.

For those at CTV and CBC who, at various times over the years, have provided an on-air home that has allowed me to share these conversations with so many, my sincere appreciation.

As I have said—as often as I possibly can—little of what I do in life would have been accomplished without the love and guidance of my family. Long ago they gave me the tools and the spirit to embark on the work that led to this book. They showed me what was right and wrong by living their values. And they instilled a genuine curiosity that has allowed me to discover life's lessons in my own way and in my own time. My sister Bonnie continues to inspire—she's one smart lady who thinks with her head and acts with heart. My father remains my wise and loving mentor. And to my mother, who hoped a broken leg might finally teach me patience, I would say, well—we can't expect miracles, Mom, but I am learning to slow down to the speed of life. Thank you for being my teacher, in the truest sense of the word. This book has given me time to think about what really matters. And, as always, it's family.

Speaking of Success

COLLECTED WISDOM,
INSIGHTS AND REFLECTIONS

Introduction

Each person's life is lived
as a series of conversations.
DEBORAH TANNEN, AUTHOR AND SOCIOLINGUIST

You know those crazy greeting cards that say "Everything I've learned in life, I've learned from ..." and then you fill in the blanks. Well, it's true. We do learn life's lessons from those around us, and almost everything I've learned in life about success—and achievement—I've found nestled in the hearts and heads of the extraordinary and eclectic collection of people whom I've had the opportunity to meet in the course of my career as a journalist and broadcaster. For nearly twenty-five years, this series of conversations has been seen on television screens across the nation. Still, despite their public airing, these exchanges have often been very personal. Believe it or not, a television studio is an intimate place. Of course the circumstance is contrived, but the substance is spontaneous, often surprising both me and the guest. I've asked questions about people's first loves and their fears about death. I've probed their pasts, explored their virtues and, on occasion, also exposed their vices.

I've dug deep to provoke the demons that haunt us all. Boxer George Chuvalo won many championships but suffered great tragedy in his personal life. As he explained, the lessons he learned in the ring helped him overcome his other difficulties: "You don't just work on your ability to administer punishment. You have to work on your ability to withstand it. I worked at both."

From each conversation I've gleaned some wisdom about life and the instinctive generosity of the human spirit. And I've learned that the true art of conversation is in the listening. In fact, I think that's the difference between interview and conversation. An interview is a series of questions asked and answered. A conversation is an exchange of ideas and the pursuit of a truth, not just the recitation of facts. As violin virtuoso Pinchas Zukerman so succinctly put it: "The listening process is what life is about."

During the course of many conversations I have recalled Tannen's valuable insight: "conversations are negotiations for closeness." I've always tried to create a comfort zone—a place where people feel willing to open up. I don't bully or intimidate. And I show respect by always doing my homework—reading their books, studying their theories or listening to their lyrics. Still, I am always amazed at people's willingness to share. This has allowed me to explore the inner world—the minds—of the rich and famous, the amazing and the courageous, the brave and the brazen, the resilient and even the reluctant. All have strived to achieve, and many have often failed along the way, but strength of character has enabled them to overcome. As a result, they are wonderful teachers.

This book is the collected wisdom, culled from thousands of hours of conversation, of some truly remarkable people. In their words, from their unique vantage points, it's a look at success and the diverse and often circuitous routes to it. These people have changed my life and they will change yours. And for the purpose of truly appreciating what follows, let me say that when I talk about success, I don't mean finding the Holy Grail of fame and fortune. It's about becoming a successful human being.

I know I am considered a successful person—mostly because I live and work on television and because our culture often sees celebrity and success as interchangeable. But I measure my success in terms of an ability to adapt and change and, when necessary, to reinvent myself. Experience has taught me that the risk and the effort are always worth it. But without my friends and family, it would not have been possible. I have a strong and supportive family, who instilled basic values and helped me set my moral compass. And my friends, some of whom date back to childhood, are intelligent, eclectic, caring and honourable. All have given me great and good guidance in life so that, in the end, I have come to measure my success by the company I keep.

Graham Kerr, the chef formerly known as the Galloping Gourmet, experienced a profound change in his life and priorities and mused aloud about his altered view. "Success is such a strange thing," he said, "I mean, how do you measure it? It's measured by rating points and usually by people looking at the bottom line. But true success, I think, is when a person changes direction—from running to a cliff and falling over to finding something of value in their own life. And they become creative." Many of us have stepped back from the brink more than once in our lives and the experience usually changes us for the better.

I've also found that the most successful human beings are often humble about their experiences. As astronaut Julie Payette told me quite genuinely: "We're simply ordinary human beings who are being given the chance to work in an extraordinary environment." Perhaps she does not see her own right stuff, but she has become, like Roberta Bondar before her, a role model. Roberta Bondar's space flight allowed the next generation—including Julie Payette and Chris Hadfield—to assume there are no barriers, gender or otherwise, to their mission.

There are others who possess specific skills that will always elude us, but their dedication and thinking can help us to focus on our own. A lovely, quiet irony could be heard in the words of the man whose team was the first to scale Mount Everest. "When we reached the summit," said Sir Edmund Hillary, "one of the thoughts I had was that we'd really only done half the job—we still had to get to the bottom again." Such matter-of-fact, rational thinking is precisely what allowed him to achieve such great heights—on the mountain and in life.

As I've listened to these accomplished people, I've heard wise words about the simple act of living life deliberately, about making our choices conscious acts. In an inspiring conversation with religious writer Jean Vanier, he talked about the "compulsion" in our society to be successful and to be admired for it. And he made a passionate plea that we think more deeply about being just and compassionate people. We're not all able to soar through space or climb mountains, but we all have the potential to be successful human beings. As the British-born biographer Nicholas Shakespeare reminded me: "We are, in the end, about eighty-eight percent water and the rest is what makes things interesting." However talented or successful we think other people are, it's important to remember that we are all more or less made of the same stuff. They, like us, have doubts and fears, and we can learn much from listening to how they have wrestled with their demons and their triumphs.

Now, as my late friend Sandra Gwyn used to say: "Ambition and love, that's what makes the world go round." But so, too, does a generosity of spirit, a belief that one must give and not just receive, and that in life and work you must be willing to think and act with both your head and your heart in play. When I asked Microsoft chairman Bill Gates about his success, he offered the words of his hero and mentor, billionaire businessman Warren Buffett, in reply—and it's a definition I love: "If success is getting what you want, then happiness is wanting what you get." And in a conversation with Pulitzer Prize–winning author Richard Ford about whether literary success had made him happy, he paused and confessed wistfully: "What would make me happy would be to write books that people found useful. Stories that contain something which, when the reader reads it, he thinks, 'Ah, I get that.'" I trust you will nod knowingly from time to time as you turn the pages of this book, and perhaps the words of others will help you see your own feelings and experiences—and potential—more clearly.

The people whose uncommon sense and wisdom grace this book's pages are those who are comfortable living out loud—people who have lived and loved and learned and know why it all matters.

This is what I share with you now. And be warned, this is not the predictable book offering a quick fix or a fast track to success and happiness. Rather, it's about what successful people have learned from the process of achieving some measure of both. There are no five easy steps or twelve quick rules to follow—just some funny, touching and remarkable moments of reflection. It is a backward glance at the human condition.

Chapter One

Setting Your
Moral Compass

*Home is where you
hang your heart.*
JANN ARDEN, SINGER AND SONGWRITER

There is nothing as comforting as that sense of home. Sometimes a song playing on the radio will trigger one of those déjà vu moments. Sometimes a smell conjures up the same sense of familiarity. And now and then, you open the pages of a book and out springs a phrase or a subtle reference that instantly transports you back in time and experience. It's an onomatopoeic moment, if there is such a thing. We remain attached to the place we call home and to the symbols and icons of it. For me, it's prairie grain elevators, saskatoon berry pie, fall suppers in church basements and Legion halls—and family.

Home is the place we learn our values. My attitudes were shaped and my value system crafted by witnessing my parents' beliefs in action. We all smile when we see a child who talks or gestures just like the parent. It is no surprise, then, that we also mimic the values we observe. It was Aristotle who wrote that moral virtues come from the habits we form in childhood. Those habits make no small difference, he said; rather, they make all the difference. And they do. For better or worse. From family I learned to set—and keep attuned to—my own moral compass, which simply means knowing right from wrong and having a sense of responsibility. So for me, home is more than just a physical place; it's a moral place, but not a moralistic one. It's the place where I learned that character always trumps genius, that being kind is more important than being smart. The writer Gail Sheehy captured it crisply in our conversation: "Character is a moral imprint on one's behaviour."

The Alberta-born singer and songwriter Jann Arden explained how strong that imprint can be:

> Whatever it is that I am, I know what makes me tick and what makes me well and what makes me happy. My father made $110 a month and bought the first house for $13,000. I remember it always took two years to pay for Christmas, and they were always two years behind on their Sears card. But I never heard my parents talk about other people having too much. I always thought I had everything, and even if we didn't, we felt we did.

Jann is always very straightforward and very funny and self-deprecating. And no matter what turn the conversation took, she always kept coming back to family. For her, family is that voice in your head reminding you about what's right and wrong:

Burdens leak into the next generation. You are not born with a blank slate.
CAROL SHIELDS, AUTHOR

My grandmother always said if you can't be good, be as good as you can be.
KIM STOCKWOOD, SINGER AND SONGWRITER

When I have a snarky day, I'm ashamed of myself if I've even remotely behaved in some way that would make my parents look at me like I'm a little brat.

When he was on the ice, Number 99 needed no advice about his next move. But when Wayne Gretzky is on home ice—stickhandling his way through the perils of fatherhood—he trusts the two most important coaches in his life:

I always do what I think my mom or my dad would think was right. And if I know they would give me the go-ahead and a yes, then I know I'm making the right decision.

It was precisely those values that a young boy from Oklahoma lost sight of when he first headed off to country music's Mecca to make his music and find fame. "The first time I moved to Nashville," explained country superstar Garth Brooks, "I knew after twenty-three hours it wasn't going to be the way I thought. I turned around and was on my way back home."

Garth explained that when he started unpacking, he realized he'd left all the things that made up "Garth Brooks" back at home:

I was leaving to do this wild thing—to get out of there and forget about everything that I had grown up with and had learned. Well, I went back home to get that. I got values—the things that you run your life on. I went back home and got loyalty and roots and then went back to Nashville two years later.

We must strive throughout our lives to live up to certain principles of kindness, morality and love that bring a certain dignity to us.

DR. SHERWIN B. NULAND, AUTHOR

I think I've spent my whole life honing in on who I am, what my purpose is and what my ideals and values are.

kd lang, SINGER AND SONGWRITER

Many of my generation, and the twenty- and thirty-somethings too, have tried to re-create—or perhaps create for the first time—that sense of belonging. The workplace and our circle of friends can often substitute for old-fashioned ideas of family and community that were missing or that we have often reluctantly left behind. Singer, songwriter, poet and painter Joni Mitchell, an only child, said this:

> My sense of family is that I have chosen it along the way. I have many brothers—blood brothers but not genetic brothers. Family is the heart.

My parents always told us to stand on our own two feet. I was made to go out and do things.

SIR RICHARD BRANSON, ENTREPRENEUR

It seems imperative to create a sense of family because the need for a comfortable cocoon where you can be yourself doesn't disappear with adulthood or a change of venue. For those of us who grew up in small towns, there was also a sense of security that perhaps came more easily because we knew everybody and no one told us not to talk to strangers, because there weren't any.

So many of my guests share my view that growing up in familiar, safe and predictable circumstances instills a self-confidence that is so important later in our adult lives and attitudes. Or as George Cohon, senior chair of McDonald's Canada, put it, your roots give you wings:

> You know your roots, where you come from, what your basic values are—and then you fly off. My parents gave them to me and I think I gave them to my children. If they pass it on to their children, that's the only obligation I want from them.

Garth Brooks echoed this idea:

> My dad is my shield and my mom is the force that allows me to
> fly. I'm a self-declared Mama's boy and I always will be.

Gloria Steinem, the outspoken feminist, made my throat close and tears well
in my eyes as she described how her parents gave her wings and her voice:

> You only know you're lovable if somebody loves you. I never
> doubted for a moment that my parents loved me. They
> respected me and they listened to me. You only know that
> you have something to say if somebody listens to you.

I've always drawn great strength from coming home.

PETER JENNINGS,
BROADCASTER AND
JOURNALIST

❧

Several times a year I make a ritual and much-needed pilgrimage to my
home in Saskatchewan for a refresher course in community, family and
the prairie version of common sense. Saskatchewan is, as the cliché goes,
a state of mind. That sense of home is very important as an anchor.
Author and playwright Timothy Findley used the same image:

> You are constantly going back home in your mind. It's as
> though the anchor could be fed out a little longer, but you're
> always attached to that one place.

I have a special place in my heart for others who share that sense of
home, people like superstar Burton Cummings:

I think as you get older, your roots mean more. And there's a comfort zone whereby I have nothing left to prove to anyone or to myself.

Burton's musical career started out in garages and basements in Winnipeg, but before long his band, the Guess Who, was topping the charts. After years on the road, Burton once again keeps a home in Winnipeg. He's been known to sit in as a DJ at a local classic rock station, and he recently purchased a restaurant, a famous hangout called The Salisbury House where he spent many late nights in his youth. When he and Randy Bachman decided to stage a reunion of the Guess Who, it was for a good cause and in the right place. If I had to bet, I'd say Winnipeg—like my hometown of Wadena—is a great leveller. As Burton said: "Winnipeg keeps me grounded when I go there, and I spend more and more time there as the years go on."

Born and raised in Nanaimo, British Columbia, jazz singer and pianist Diana Krall is another small-town girl whose family remains her anchor. We spent much of our conversation on the importance, as she expressed it, of a "very strong, solid family with a clear idea of who we are." The last time Diana and I spoke, her mother, Adella, had battled and survived cancer. And through it all, Diana said, Adella never lost her "glass is half full" view of the world: "My mother is like a little Buddha—you know, 'The barn burned down so now I can see the moon.' That's her whole attitude."

Actress Michele Lee is one of those irrepressibly enthusiastic people. The woman many of you knew as Karen on all 344 episodes

You only get one hometown.
BURTON CUMMINGS,
SINGER AND SONGWRITER

of the television drama *Knots Landing* bounded into the studio, eager to talk and extol the virtues of family. She credits family with allowing her to find success and keep her head about her: "We are who we are because of the people that have touched us." And sometimes that's quite literally true, because it is touch that so often gives us comfort. Jason Sniderman, son of the legendary Sam the Record Man, shared his experience:

> The greatest lesson I learned from my father is never hide your emotions from your kids. My father and I still kiss each other every day. And I couldn't last a day without kissing my kids.

For many of my guests who have enjoyed—or endured—the pressure of fame, family is a reality check. It is for Jann Arden:

> I think sometimes when you're dealing with yourself all the time, it's easy for things to get away from you. And I'm aware of that. Your friends and family keep you humble.

Terri Clark is another of the crop of New Country singing stars, also from Alberta, and she shares Jann's view:

> You have to remember your roots and where you came from and who you really are, or you're going to become something that you're not and that's the last thing in the world I ever want to happen. If the hat gets too small, I'm out the door.

I think I'm a good friend because I have such good friends. My dad always says you become what your friends are.
JANN ARDEN, SINGER AND SONGWRITER

It is said that if you want to know a person's true character, don't ask him to tell you his creed or his code because we all have a set piece that can be trotted out for public consumption. Instead, ask him to tell you which living person he most admires, because hero worship is the truest index of a person's private nature. So it's a question I always put to my guests, including former football star and now coach Michael "Pinball" Clemons, who had this to say:

> My mother is really my hero. We came from a very modest background. She was a leader by example. Single parent at eighteen, full-time job, and she had to care for my great-great-grandmother. Still, she found time to help other people out. First of all, she didn't neglect her responsibility for me by pushing me off to someone else, then she took care of my great-great-grandmother, then, over and above that, she was always helping someone else, always the one to try and lend a hand. She led by example and she was a wonderful role model.

For Canadian Peter Jennings, the respected anchor of ABC's *World News Tonight*, it was his dad—also a broadcaster—who was his role model:

> My father was probably my only hero and I remember almost daily some of his very basic rules about fairness, equity and letting the audiences judge for themselves—and don't stick your opinions down other people's throats.

I think we need heroes desperately.

SIR RICHARD
ATTENBOROUGH, FILMMAKER

When I asked Catherine Clark, daughter of Progressive Conservative leader Joe Clark and lawyer Maureen McTeer, about her heroes, without missing a beat she said:

> My mom and dad. I admire them very much. My father always remains constant in his convictions regardless of what other people are saying. And my mother has been so steadfast through it all and it's not been easy. She's really shown the way for me.

My mother's gift was one of imagination
PAT CONROY, AUTHOR

In a most eloquent tribute to parents and family, here's what Leacock Medal for Humour–winning author Paul Quarrington told me:

> You can draw certain parallels between looking for God and parenthood. One of the conclusions you might come to about God is that he merely sets things in motion and is confident in the way things are going to turn out and then removes himself from the picture. And you equate that with "the best thing I can do as a parent is maybe set things in motion, see what they learn and remove myself from the picture."

As a young girl, Monique Bégin never once played with a toy. Her family were refugees fleeing the war. She went on to become Canada's Health and Welfare minister in three parliaments in the seventies and eighties and authored the Canada Health Act. After leaving politics, she became the dean of Health Sciences at the University of

Ottawa, an institution with which she is still affiliated. When the Krever Commission was investigating the tainted blood scandal, the Honourable Monique Bégin came forward, even though she was long out of power and not expected to take political responsibility. When I asked her why, she said it was how she was raised:

> What guides me is a childhood sense of justice. You know, kids at school have an absolute sense of justice. Nothing is negotiable. It's almost a black-and-white proposal. I get it from my dad. My dad was always like that. I'm offended when justice is offended. It's genetic.

I wondered how these values had been reflected in her decision to leave the political stage. She smiled and shrugged and said, "I didn't love power enough." Her clear sense of right and wrong had squelched the necessary killer instinct.

Harmony comes from clear priorities.

Jean Vanier,
humanitarian

❧

In a great number of the conversations I have had about family, mothers seem to play a profound role in the lives of many of the people who have gone on to find or create success. Juliette, "Our Pet," whose face and voice graced television screens every Saturday night after *Hockey Night in Canada* for more than a decade, ended every show with the same phrase: "Good night Mom. Good night everybody." Now in her seventies, Juliette—who looks as gorgeous as ever—still pays tribute to her mother: "She was the light of my life. I loved her very much."

One of the wittiest accolades from daughter to mother came from the actress and model Isabella Rossellini. Her mother, of course, was screen legend Ingrid Bergman, a woman who revered practicalities and instilled that reverence in her daughter.

> The most important thing I learned from my mother was cleaning. Cleaning gives me a high. I think it is soothing. It makes me feel at peace to know that my closet is all in order.

I find the same thing—those little habits we watched our mothers repeat somehow took hold, almost by osmosis. I'm sure some of us hammer just the way our dads did. I do, complete with the most foul list of four-letter words you can imagine when the nails don't automatically enter the wall at the perfect angle.

My kids saw me be happy at what I do and they saw a work ethic. They saw me work and saw me enjoy it.
Comedian Carl Reiner

Jane Goodall, the world-renowned primatologist, had her mother's unconditional support to go out into the world and do what women had not done before. Even when she was a young girl, Jane's interests—including a fascination with collecting worms— were in the outdoors. Her mother would never throw out the worms that her young daughter had stashed in her room. Instead, Jane recalled, she just patiently explained that "they'll soon be dead if they don't have the earth." Her mother had a lot to do with who Jane became:

> I credit my mother with who I am today and what I've done today, because when I was passionately in love with Tarzan, determined to go to Africa when I was ten years old and

terribly jealous of Tarzan's Jane, and thinking she was a wimp and I could be ever such a better mate for Tarzan myself, all her friends said to [my mother], "Why don't you tell Jane to dream about something she can achieve?" And my mother would say, "Jane, if you really want something, you work hard, you take advantage of opportunities, you never give up, you will find a way." I wanted to go to Africa and I did.

An eighteen year old wrote in his diary, "The United Nations is my destiny." That young boy was Maurice Strong, now senior adviser to the Secretary General of the U.N. and to the president of the World Bank. He recalls: "My mother very early on inculcated in me an interest in the larger world, and I wanted to be part of that world." Maurice Strong is considered a true citizen of the world, and with that status comes both power and influence. He's run major companies such as Petro-Canada and Power Corporation. He advises CEOs, presidents and prime ministers and finds time to act as director of the World Economic Forum Foundation, as chair of the Stockholm Environment Institute and of the Earth Council, and as president of the United Nations University for Peace in Costa Rica. He also, you may remember, organized the Earth Summit in Rio de Janeiro—and the leaders came. Growing up in Oak Lake, Manitoba, he learned a life lesson about the importance of making a contribution—from his mother:

My mother really taught me something when she said, "You won't know when to stop, until something stops you. So just keep going. Just keep moving. Do what you can do. And don't set limits for yourself. There are limits, but don't set them in advance. You'll find them when you encounter them." And I'm still looking for them.

Chapter Two

Making It Matter

*Between the cradle and the grave there's a journey and people
are searching for something.*
ROBERT DUVALL, ACTOR

In his working life, Robert Duvall has played some incredible roles—in *The Godfather*, *Tender Mercies*, the *Lonesome Dove* series and, of course, in *Apocalypse Now* as the insane Commander Kilgour. I'll never forget his line about loving the smell of napalm in the morning. When Duvall visited our studios, he had just completed the movie *The Apostle*, a brutally honest look at Bible-thumping preachers and televangelists and at how spectacle overwhelms the substance of their religious beliefs. The project was a labour of love and took fifteen years to complete. When it was rejected by the major studios, Duvall eventually bankrolled the film himself. He had always wanted to tell stories that mattered, but despite his good intentions, it seemed unlikely he'd have the chance. His first play received such horrendous reviews that it closed on opening night. Duvall recalled his early years:

After that, I took many jobs, then I got a job at the post office—the first time I'd ever had money in my pocket. At the end of six months, I thought, I've got to quit. If I don't, I'll be here twenty years from now. It was tough, at first, but I started to get a bit of acting work and then it snowballed.

For Duvall, being alive and "being emotional," he says, are the only things that matter:

There's always a learning process, and the older I get, I always want to think of myself as in the potential—always getting better. Searching.

Singer and songwriter Loreena McKennitt shared a similar view about the constant search:

So much of what we do seems to lack purpose. Yes, of course we must work in order to pay the mortgage or educate the kids or take that trip. But what is our greater objective? Sometimes our work can lead us closer to that purpose.

For many of us, it is indeed our work that gives us definition and identity and, if you are lucky or determined, a sense of purpose. For others, it's their faith or their relationships. But whatever the starting point, we are looking for ways to deal with what philosopher Mark Kingwell—a frequent and always eloquent guest—calls a meaning deficit: "People want their lives to mean something and want to be able to contribute in meaningful ways." Time and again I ask the question: How do we conquer the meaning deficit in our work? This question is at the heart of the matter and is the motivation for inviting the guests I do, because those I seek out have said or done something that intrigues me and suggests they have turned their mind to the big questions—and the search for the meaning of life. Maurice Strong told me he's turned down many "jobs" in his life, in search of meaningful work:

Fame has never been that important to me that I'll just sell my soul to get it.
CHARLIE MAJOR, MUSICIAN

> If I was simply looking at the job, I wouldn't have conducted my life the way I have. I am interested in what I am doing. I am interested in the substance of what I'm doing … Instead of despairing, wouldn't it be a lot more exciting to invent some solutions?

For forty years, Graham Kerr was the much-watched, much-loved chef and entertainer the Galloping Gourmet. But after a contract dispute, he and his wife gave up the Galloping Gourmet name and the show, severed all contacts, sold their house and their belongings, piled into a station wagon and headed off to see if they could discover what really mattered:

> I earned a lot of money and owned a lot of things. They were so important to who I was that those things really had to go away so I could be who I am.

Kerr was happy and relaxed throughout our conversation, barely mentioning the new cookbook he was selling. He was back on TV, with his own show dedicated to healthy living. As he described his new minimalist approach to life, I mused aloud that we've all fantasized about running away from it all only to discover, in the cold light of day, that there are bills to be paid, commitments to be kept and work to be done. So, I asked, any second thoughts? Kerr replied:

> No regrets whatsoever. I would have regrets if I were still wandering around in a ten-thousand-square-foot mansion house. I wouldn't know how to do it. We live on our sailboat and we're building a fourteen-hundred-square-foot house. We wanted to know how to live within reason—at the end of an unreasonable age. We spent thirty years buying stuff and then having garage sales. Now, we really would love to be relational and have time for one another. My wife, Trina, is a poet and an artist, and I want her to be able to paint and write and I want to be supportive of that and I want to help wherever I can help and do whatever I can do, and that's it.

And once he'd found himself, he said, he also found his faith:

> I used to talk about the poor a great deal. In fact, a bishop of the Anglican Church asked me if I would go on tour of the United States because I had—apparently—a profound message

Words are one thing. Actions are another.

SARAH FERGUSON,
DUCHESS OF YORK

42

about feeding the poor. But I had never given a penny. I suppose the major thing that happened to me was that I was familiar with saying nice things and then, halfway through my life, I became familiar with doing nice things. And I was not quite so fussed about gathering brownie points for me but in being more involved with the reality of reaching someone else.

Kerr's story is a dramatic one. But whatever route they take, a growing number of the people I meet want to make their lives less encumbered and more relevant. Pollster Michael Adams, a friend as well as a continuous font of information, explained why:

> Baby boomers are fifty. Mortality looms. They're looking for meaning. What are they going to do? They are not going back to the church—there's no priest with enough time to listen to all their sins. They are going to have to find meaning in another way.

For Moishe Safdie, the Canadian architect who teaches at Harvard and was, among many other triumphs, the visionary creator of Habitat in Montreal and the National Gallery in Ottawa, work must be for a greater good:

> I think a social conscience is what differentiates architects who are committed to the welfare of the people who will use the

Pay attention to the particulars of your life, ask yourself what you're doing, see what it is, what kind of compromises you can make.
RICHARD FORD, AUTHOR

buildings and those architects who think of the buildings as abstract sculpture or as a vehicle for self-expression. I belong to the first group, and I feel that that is the future of architecture. Any architecture that's going to be meaningful has to grow from the needs and dreams of people and can't be just a narcissistic self-obsession.

There are those whose mission it is to change the world. Anita Roddick created The Body Shop in 1976. "We had a voice, we were outraged, we were activists and we brought our hearts to the workplace," she told me. Now there are seventeen hundred stores selling environmentally friendly products in forty-nine countries. Her staff share her dream:

> Most of the people I employ want to be part of a social experiment. They want to change the way things are. They don't measure wealth by miles of road, or barrels of oil—they are influenced by music; they are looking for heroes and heroines amongst themselves; they want to feel good; they want an experiential education.

The global businesswoman, whose personal fortune is estimated at US$150 million, is an ardent voice in the antiglobalization movement and uses her wealth to make a difference in the causes she chooses. The money is simply a means to the end.

Pure pragmatism destroys you.
Henry Kissinger, diplomat

You have to concentrate on the work, you can't concentrate on the money, you can't concentrate on the success.
Jack Klugman, actor

You need to do essentially what you would do for nothing and then figure out a way to make a living doing it. GIL BELLOWS, ACTOR

It was the joy of the work, the discovery. I didn't do it to get paid. I did it because I loved it. If you care about your work and work hard at it, it will stand by you. It's what gave me an education. It's my best friend and it's always been loyal to me. JACK KLUGMAN, ACTOR

You can't have literature without mission. Essentially, what you are is an entertainer, but if you're really good, you've got to motivate them. You've got to be a bit of a preacher, and I come from a long line of preachers. FARLEY MOWAT, AUTHOR

Garth Brooks was a phenomenon that almost defied explanation. He is, without question, extremely talented. And he seemed to be the right voice at the right time. His concerts were spectacles and always sold out, his CD sales were breaking records. As we talked about his success, I noticed he kept referring to himself in the third person or as "we":

Garth Brooks isn't this guy. Garth Brooks is that crew who are up at five in the morning and it's the people who come. This is a gig I have—and I can't waste it. Part of this gig is having fun, but with it also comes a responsibility. You have to say things that you believe in, and I believe that my purpose is to let people know that they are not alone in how they are feeling. I want to actually cause an emotion—good or bad. I wish I could explain this to you. It's the greatest gift—and the greatest gig—that God ever gave anybody. It's what life is for me.

For Garth, it's the audience that matters most in his work: "The ultimate judge shouldn't be who's singing it, it should be who's hearing it."

For the "creative" person, loving the work you do seems to go with the territory. You don't become a painter or a writer against your will, and so if you are an artist or an actor or a musician, it may be easier to be passionate about what you do. But I think there are lessons for all of us in finding something that—at the very least—gives us a sense of satisfaction or of being part of something that makes people's lives safer or healthier or easier or happier. Oscar-winning filmmaker Norman Jewison made it clear he doesn't do message movies. Tugging at his trademark baseball cap and grinning, he said he's not out to convert us, only to challenge our thinking and his own talent. "If you're going to spend a year of your life at something, it better have some meaning for you," he advised.

When people come to a show, they can tell the difference between somebody who is pretending to like what they do ... and when they really do.

TERRI CLARK, SINGER

～

I hope I love my music. You'd better be proud of the work you create or you're going to have a hard time sleeping. KIM STOCKWOOD, SINGER

As an actor, I've become a true amateur in that I do it because I love it now. ANN-MARIE MACDONALD, NOVELIST, PLAYWRIGHT, ACTOR

I just want to spend the rest of my working life writing plays. It makes no difference to me whether they go to Broadway or not. NEIL SIMON, PULITZER PRIZE–WINNING PLAYWRIGHT

～～

I always ask my guests the questions I'm asking myself: Why do you do what you do? What motivates you? Do you still love your work? Does it challenge you and use your ingenuity and brains? As political satirist and author P.J. O'Rourke quite rightly pointed out, we do need some incentive to get up in the morning:

> People are not going to work and get nothing out of work—they're not crazy. Now they don't have to get money exactly. There's one school of economics called Public Choice Economics, it's brilliant. The thesis is, everybody gets paid.

When I attach myself to something I love, then I'm the luckiest man in the world.
MARVIN HAMLISCH, COMPOSER

Mother Teresa got paid. They may not always get paid with money. They may get paid with power, prestige, with eternal salvation, but everybody gets paid. Nobody works without a purpose—of course they don't. We all know that. Maybe we work for love, but we have to work for something.

Whatever we do, we can only hope that we love what we do because most of us spend far more time at work than we do with our intimate partners or families. And then there's the unsettling fact, shared by self-help guru Deepak Chopra, that the decisions we make about how we spend our working time may truly be a matter of life and death. The statistics tell us that more people die in Western civilizations at nine o'clock on Monday morning than at any other time. Job dissatisfaction is the number one predictor of heart disease, and people who hate their jobs are the ones who are most susceptible.

In 1949, Ed McMahon, who later became Johnny Carson's straight man, was a pitchman on the boardwalk in Atlantic City selling the Mars Metric Slicer and making a thousand dollars a week. He gave it up for a job on TV at seventy-five dollars a week. He told me, "You couldn't keep me out of this business at gunpoint … I'm so lucky I can make a living at what I love."

John Le Carré, spymaster and writer of superior thrillers, has penned a lifetime of bestsellers and has earned more than enough money for comfort and ease:

Money is grotesque and it doesn't satisfy. I think there is a limit to our interest in material goods. As Groucho Marx said when he wrote a successful book, "Now I can have a typewriter for each finger."

Most of us fool ourselves into thinking that if we had bundles of money, we'd give up our jobs and the daily grind. But few of the people I've talked with over the years would—even if they could—choose that path, including Pulitzer Prize–winning author Frank McCourt. He used to dream that if he wrote a bestseller he'd "sit on his behind" in some exotic location. Instead, he kept on writing and teaching, and he warns that freedom does not necessarily come with money:

> My book, *Angela's Ashes*, has made millions, but now I have to have an investment adviser, a lawyer, a bookkeeper—it's so boring. But then you have to say, "What am I going to do with the money?" I haven't much time left. But I have to do something with it. The Bible says, though, "To whom much is given, much is expected."

G. Scott Paterson, chair and CEO of Yorkton Securities Inc., one of the largest independent investment houses on Toronto's Bay Street, is someone to whom much has been given:

> Some days I think I should go to a mountaintop and yell out "*Yahoo!*" because I have been very lucky in life. I've worked very hard for it, too, I'd like to think. It's not about money to me. At the end of the day, I'd do this for a lot less money.

There's nothing like a little fear or a little hunger to challenge one's inspiration, and to take that away from a young artist is not necessarily doing them a favour.

KEN DANBY, ARTIST

His perspective comes from a lesson learned early:

> I remember some dark days. A company I started lost money
> heavily. I had a negative self-worth and I wondered how I was
> going to climb out. My shirts had holes in them—I could not
> afford a new shirt. We ate grilled cheese sandwiches and took
> the cable TV back because we needed the ten dollars a month.
> But it was one of the best learning experiences of my whole
> life. It actually took me away from a money and material focus.
> I really realized I needed goals in life that weren't about
> money. I had to face the reality that I might never make a lot
> of money. More or less, the day that I decided that money
> truly wasn't the driving force, then money started coming in.
> So there's a lot to be said to make sure you don't focus on
> the money.

*It's not the money. But
what's the point of living
if you don't do something
great?*

Dr. Morty Shulman,
broadcaster

And what you are worth to society is not necessarily reflected by your
net worth or annual income. Scott Paterson knows:

> I reflect upon how lucky I am. It's not necessarily fair. There
> are many people in our society who contribute a great deal and
> simply because of the vocation they have chosen are not
> rewarded financially.

Former Supreme Court of Canada justice Willard (Bud) Estey is
in his eighties and still goes to his law office every day. He was a guest

on one program about making it matter after eighty, and what got the judge's blood boiling was a discussion about whether we respect—and are willing to pay for—the wisdom that our elders bring to the table. Estey told me this:

> Somebody else once said, "Knowledge comes but wisdom lingers." Nobody pays for wisdom—they pay for knowledge, maybe. But wisdom is an egotistical two-way equation. The recipient doesn't think it is wisdom, and the fellow that utters it thinks it is the last word. There is no payoff in life unless you've got the energy and the imagination and the sense that it's all a game and to keep going—it's got to be something that involves your ingenuity and your brains.

Actor Christopher Plummer put it another way:

> If you get too successful and too rich and too well fed, you're in danger, in this business, of losing all the things that you had when you were not so rich and working your way up the ladder.

Well, no danger of that for me. I've always been downwardly mobile, financially speaking. While my career—a word that implies more planning than I've ever done—appears to be very successful, I certainly could have made much more money by heading south of the border. A Canadian passport and our good training make us good

I never thought I would make a living, I thought I would have to work at something else just so I could do this.

JACK KLUGMAN, ACTOR

candidates for jobs on U.S. TV networks. But I loved the Canadian story, our country and our journalistic freedoms and attitudes. When it comes to work, Canadians, it seems, don't just do it for the money, according to pollster Michael Adams. Still, money is often how we measure success and worth:

> How we make it, how we spend it and how we give it away is where the rubber hits the road when it comes to expressing our values.

⌘

Get away from empty heroes and people that just look good or just play a game well. To me, this is not enough to be a hero. You have to change somebody's life.

Neil Peart, musician

When I was a young girl, we saved dimes out of our allowance and put them in little cardboard containers. Somehow these dimes magically helped put food in the mouths of starving children—in some unimaginable and unpronounceable far-flung nation. At the supper table, if we balked at some vegetable or prodded our stew in search of clues to the true identity of the various bits and pieces, my parents would admonish us to clean up our plates, count our blessings and think about those starving children—whose faces we'd never seen. (This was, of course, the pre-CNN era). My parents were both products of the Depression and wartime rationing, so, despite their two steady incomes, there was always a sense of being thankful for what you've got and a rule about always eating what was put in front of you because you never knew where the next meal was coming from. We were taught to think about those less fortunate than ourselves. Mom used to pack extra sandwiches in the lunch box so we could share them. And I remember a friend's mother who used to say, "If you have no shoes, look at someone with no feet." These were crucial lessons about understanding the differences between need and want, and about our responsibilities to the community at large. It was, come to think of it, a very global view, long before we knew about globalization and even before Marshall McLuhan talked about the shrinking global village.

I had the opportunity to meet someone who has taken all those lessons to heart, who sees himself as a citizen of the world and who has willingly risked his life in the places where the boxes of dimes were destined to go. When I first spoke with Dr. Chris Giannou, he had just returned to Canada from his latest tour of duty as a war surgeon—one of the most highly respected in the world—with the International Committee of the Red Cross. For seventeen years, in places like Lebanon, Chechnya, Cambodia and Somalia, the battlefield surgeon dispensed salvation, he told me, with varying degrees of competence and success. Still, Chris believes one person can make a difference:

> I don't think of myself as a missionary. A crusader, maybe. I have very strong beliefs and my own system of values. I think, rather than explaining what one's values are, in which case one tends to fall into traps of rhetoric, you *do*. You *live* your values. Even if it means certain personal sacrifices, certain personal dangers that you run, you live it.

His words make you realize just how important it is to bring your values to the workplace. How else will we shape the values of organizations

The whole of the mystery is that every person has a mission.

JEAN VANIER, HUMANITARIAN

or of our societies if we don't put into practice what we believe? But as Chris pointed out, values are not the same as biases:

> If you want to pick a side, don't sign up for humanitarian aide. Go and be a part of the conflict and maintain your integrity. You have to show by your actual actions in the field that you are impartial in front of the victim, you are neutral towards the belligerent. As a doctor, impartiality towards the victim is easy—it's medical ethics. I'll have several people in front of me who are ill or wounded. My decision on their treatment is based on medical need, not on the colour of their skin, their language, their religion, their ethnic background, et cetera.

Every project I go into, I go in pure of heart and strong-willed and with an open mind and then hope for the best beyond that.

Joe Mantegna, actor

As our public conversation continued, I was holding a private conversation with myself inside my head. It was not driven by guilt, nor is that what Chris intended to provoke. As he said, you can't regulate compassion. Rather, his words were sparking a review of my own beliefs and behaviours—toward the homeless on the street, toward refugees, political and economic, who arrive in leaky ships and lethal containers. Could I suspend my biases in making my choices about whom and where to help? I'm sure the gruesome reality in which Chris works displaces the luxury of such debate.

For years Chris carried around a tattered copy of a book by the French novelist and philosopher Albert Camus. Camus says there is only one real philosophical question that must be asked each day: Why shouldn't I commit suicide today? The answer, of course, is your reason for living. For a war-zone doctor surrounded by death, the reason is, in part, the small satisfaction he finds in cheating it. Chris's tone was almost steely as he explained:

> I do not save lives; I delay death. The person I operated on today may not die today, but he will eventually die. In that postponing, I give that person the joys of life—but also the time to go through the other suffering.

Then Chris softened slightly and added:

> We all have constraints. I can only operate on one person at a time. I can only work in certain places with some people part of the time. Those are limits. The important thing is to recognize one's limits, I think. And it's in that recognition that you can then, at times, overcome even your own limits.

It's almost like a mantra to me: It doesn't matter. Just keep an eye on what does matter.

ANN MEDINA, JOURNALIST
AND FILMMAKER

Dr. Giannou has chosen a life that has given him many rewards but few material goods. At one point he arrived back in Canada with a toothbrush as his only personal possession. He reflected on this situation:

> I thought, I have only a toothbrush. But I am alive, there are a lot of people who are dead. I am whole, there are a lot of people who have lost a limb. I am free, I have colleagues in prison. I am out, and there are a lot of people still on the battlefield facing death and violence. Well, a toothbrush suits me just fine.

Being Your
Brother's Keeper

"Commune," coming together. That's what community means. It really is an insurance policy. The whole concept of an insurance policy is a bunch of people putting in so that when someone has a problem—death or sickness—then the policy kicks in. And that's what community is all about: We all try to help each other out and then, when it's our turn, you know someone else is there.
MICHAEL "PINBALL" CLEMONS, FOOTBALL STAR

What a great description—community as insurance policy. I like the idea of injecting a little self-interest into the whole equation if it allows people to buy in. The enlightened self-interest of those with power has always been a great motivator for change in society. So too is the belief that one can make a difference in the lives of many.

If community is supposed to be about shared values and priorities and about what we can do for ourselves collectively, then our large urban centres can be frustrating environments. Being alone together is not a community, it's a city. People live "as neighbours" largely because of their ability to afford similar accommodation, and it's hard to share values—or even know if you do—if your accommodation is the only common denominator. As for shared priorities, that may have more to do with regular garbage collection than with the importance of family or faith or music or friends in one's life.

If nostalgia doesn't help us deal with today's urban realities, perhaps the wise words of a football star may serve as an incentive. For Pinball, it is faith that shapes his world view. For crusading author Farley Mowat, it's the need for a sense of belonging. Human nature is such that we seem to want to be part of something larger—a family, a couple, a team or a community. And Farley believes that when it comes to community, size matters:

> I am a tribalist. I believe in a small community where everything done is for the good of the tribe. Ninety-nine percent of us have been de-tribalized. We only have artificial tribes—clubs, associations, even states or provinces—but they are all artificial. I've been looking for my tribe my whole life. You have to be born into it. You can't fabricate it. The Internet, for example, will not create a tribe.

The Internet can create communities of interest, but we may be losing the physical communities that Farley talks about. Local needs can so easily disappear when we live in an increasingly global world. Real-time television and all-news channels make it easier—and more urgent—to relate to a war or disaster an ocean away than to be aware of the woman next door who may need a meal or a friend. All the more reason, Farley pronounced, to remember that community is a

You have to make up your mind whether you want to be a party of one or whether you want to be one of a party.

<small>DALTON CAMP, COLUMNIST</small>

My mother used to teach us that you lived in a community—and you don't just take from the community, you give back.

<small>AL WAXMAN, ACTOR</small>

place where responsibilities—and not just rights—still matter: "Tribes are their brother's keeper and they are strong."

I was just reading Eric Kierans's memoir *Remembering*, which is wonderfully eloquent on the whole idea of community. But the most forceful chapter is his final one, "The Cain Culture." It begins with a quote from the biblical story of brothers Cain and Abel:

> And the Lord said unto Cain, Where is Abel thy brother?
> And he said, I know not: Am I my brother's keeper?

Kierans says that that is the single most important question that has ever been asked because it is a question that covers all aspects of living and meaning, and all spheres of activity—the political and the economic, the social and the cultural and, of course, the spiritual and the moral.

When the former moderator of the United Church, the Right Reverend Bill Phipps, was a guest on the program, he said the answer to Cain's question must always be yes:

> The Bible is concerned with our economic relationships—the gap between rich and poor. If you look at the Final Judgment that Jesus talks about in Matthew 25, it's about how we clothe the naked, feed the hungry, welcome the refugee and the stranger into our homes—that could have been written yesterday morning. It has to do with how we live together as a community.

We have to have a strong commitment to personal responsibility. I don't want to live in a society where people give up on looking after their old folk. We have obligations to look after our parents, we have obligations to look after our children.

MICHAEL IGNATIEFF,

AUTHOR

Hugh Segal, a long-time political commentator and head of the Institute for Research on Public Policy, expressed the idea this way:

> The whole advent of the gated community—the notion that we can live within the walls of our community and we will be safe and, beyond the walls, that's not our problem—isn't right. Actually, beyond the walls is everybody's problem. We're all part of this family and we have to reach out and be constructive in this regard. The concept of community implies a series of things: respect for differences, respect for pluralism and respect for dissent.

For years I have watched my sister, Bonnie, put her pragmatic views into action. Motivated by a firm belief that we are each the keeper of our community, she was determined to rescue the lost causes of the world—those who had been shunted off to mental institutions straight out of *One Flew Over the Cuckoo's Nest*. Bonnie believes that the mentally challenged have plenty of untapped potential—and humanity. So, in our hometown of Wadena, Saskatchewan, she has helped forty or so mentally and physically challenged clients build a sense of community while becoming part of the larger one. Irene and Neil help run a catering service for banquets and dinners, and Johanna is in charge of a major recycling project that, when it began, was a pilot for the entire province. Jerry works in the shoe repair, Neil and Dale use sophisticated tools to manufacture wood pallets for shipping, and Betty Ann is part of the team that is recycling computers (although, because of her fascination with the alphabet, she's been known to pocket a few of the keys with the Bs on them). Others work at jobs in the community—Carol at the bakery, Brenda at the laundromat and Clayton at the landfill site. Most live in group homes and some now live independently. They can do this because they belong to a community.

Perhaps my sister's work is the reason I connected so powerfully with Jean Vanier. Few of the conversations any of us have with strangers would qualify as "inspirational." Even in the course of my work, seldom do I have the time to delve deep enough to discover such wisdom. Vanier's life and his writing, including *Becoming Human*, is the search for what makes a successful human being. It's an anthropological look at human nature, a view that resulted from living with and observing those with no artifice. Let me explain it to you as he did to me.

In 1964, after years in the military followed by a career teaching philosophy and studying theology, Vanier, the son of Canada's late governor general, Georges Vanier, and his wife, Pauline, began visiting asylums that housed the mentally handicapped. The screams and the sadness Jean Vanier witnessed soon turned his anguish into action. He bought a ramshackle house in Trosly-Breuil in France and invited two mentally handicapped men, Phillipe Seux and Raphael Simi, to live with him—permanently. He named their home L'Arche, after Noah's ark, and it became the inspiration for the more than one hundred such Christian communities that now exist around the world, where the mentally challenged live with their caregivers. For him, Vanier said, this was an irreversible act. L'Arche has become both vocation and home.

Some problems—spiritual and moral—do not have a political solution.
LEWIS LAPHAM, EDITOR, HARPER'S

Vanier has been called a saint, a prophet, the greatest living philanthropist and even "the male Mother Teresa." If you don't worship him, you don't know him, say those who do. But of all the descriptions of this man, the one that rang true for me was "vivid." You feel his presence. He touches you because he's an uncommon example of selflessness in a selfish world. I began our conversation by asking Vanier this question: "If God is good and God is great, why did he create people with brains that don't work in the way we understand to be normal?" This is how he answered:

> If God is good and God is great, why did he create people who don't listen to them? The problem is not with those people. The problem is with us. Why are we putting them in asylums when they are beautiful people? It's because we don't want them. The problem with humanity is prejudice. Prejudice and fear because we don't want people like that. And why don't we? Because they are calling us to change and to change our value systems.

Vanier believes that the human heart must be liberated from fear so that we can begin to discover our common humanity. God has chosen the weak to confound the strong, said Vanier, noting that the weak have been his best teachers in life. He is fond of telling the story of Antonio, a man who spent twenty years in various institutions before coming to L'Arche. He can't walk or talk or use his hands to any effect; but when people address him by name, his face lights up. There is no depression or anger in that man, said Vanier, despite his condition. And when Antonio's caregivers are asked how Antonio is doing at L'Arche, they answer that he has transformed them:

> As soon as you meet someone who is down and out, you enter into a heartfelt relationship. Live with people who have been crushed, begin to listen to them, and you will be changed. Climb down off your pedestal, become a friend, open your heart and let's celebrate life. Have fun. I believe what we have to come back to is a sense of community. And by community I mean a network of friends.

Can any of us make the effort and sacrifice and commitment required to connect with those in need? Vanier believes it's a simpler proposition than you think:

> As human beings open up, they become interested in the world around them and then they desire to work for the collective good. We must move from a world in which we are just clutching on to what we need to a world where we are discovering the needs of others. They can help us. They teach us something about life.

Not everyone needs to create or move to a L'Arche community to have an impact. We have plenty of needs to be met here at home. I have had the good fortune to meet others who are doing just that.

Anybody who is doing well—not just successful financially, but is in good health—should be giving back. People need it instilled at an early age how they are going to make their contribution.
SCOTT PATERSON,
BUSINESSMAN

They share Vanier's passion and they live the words they speak.

Tom Jackson is a handsome and talented actor and singer. His husky, deeper-than-the-ocean voice is powerful and, at almost six and a half feet tall, he is a commanding presence. But it's Tom's quiet commitment to changing lives that is truly compelling:

Twenty percent of the population cannot survive on its own and it's the obligation of the other eighty percent to look after that twenty percent, and that's the whole story.
SENATOR SISTER PEGGY BUTTS

I think a lot of the people we think have less, have more. There's a lot of light in those people who have less. I toast the people who have less who make us do more. My life would be meaningless without all those people. People who give me reason to live. And we should pay attention. We're all on common ground.

Tom had a great family life, growing up off the reserve. But as a teenager, he took to the streets, making his way as a pool hustler. When I probed for the details, all he'd say was that before long he was in serious trouble and a Salvation Army volunteer stepped in to stop his downward slide. As one who was down and out, he found himself one night about to step over a man who lay dying in the street. Instead of passing him by, Tom stopped to help.

Some people would suggest I saved his life, but he saved mine and changed my way of thinking. How would you feel if you were lying there and people were walking by you— and you were dying, or thought you were. I can't bear that thought.

66

Tom wishes we could all stop walking by and realize that we, too, could be just a paycheque—or a few drinks—away from the same fate. He simply tries to lead by example and show us there is no "us" and "them":

> It's my attempt to try and make homeless people become human beings to the rest of the world—same as Native people. Native people are not "they," Native people are "we." We are human beings, regardless of colour, what we look like or how we talk. We have the same problems—you and I.

Tom dedicates the proceeds from his Huron Carol Christmas concerts and albums to the Canadian Association of Food Banks:

> A lot of the stuff I do is self-indulgent. I do things for other people, but it's really me feeling good about doing it. I encourage other people to do it because it's a great addiction. There are great addictions out there—you don't have to be addicted to bad things. People say overindulgence [in] anything can be destructive. Naw. Kill 'em with kindness and you can't lose.

Increasingly we know fewer and fewer people that are unlike ourselves.

LEWIS LAPHAM, EDITOR, HARPER'S

Tom claims that kindness to strangers has made his life worthwhile and him a better performer:

> It strikes me that it was my work with the homeless that ultimately made me concentrate on my career as an actor and as a singer so that I could continue this work, so I owe a lot to this.

And that's the thing about giving back. All who make giving a part of their life agree that, in many ways, it's an act of selfishness— that the giver is rewarded every bit as much as the recipient. Pinball Clemons agreed:

> It all is a many-splendoured thing when it all comes together. Giving back gives me more than I'll ever be able to give. I think Ralph Waldo Emerson said it best when he said, "One of the most beautiful compensations in life is this: No man can sincerely try to help another without helping himself." The true joy in life, I believe, comes from giving.

Set your objectives and become accountable, not to the governments or to the organizations, but to the objectives that meet the needs of the community.
RICK HANSEN, ACTIVIST

The gregarious, and generous, CEO of McDonald's Canada, George Cohon, is also unabashed in his enthusiasm for the belief that giving back is a duty:

> Day one when I got involved with McDonald's I said, "Put something back into the communities you operate in." I think, in this day and age, if you're fortunate enough to be successful, then you have an absolute duty to put as much back in as you can. Why do I wake up every morning and go to work at McDonald's, why do I get involved with the Santa Claus Parade or the Science Centre or the hospital board? It's your duty to society. You're part of society. You exist because of society. I'm healthy enough to do it and I want to keep

doing it. It makes my life seem worthwhile. All of the other stuff seems unimportant to me now. It's wonderful stuff to do. I am what I am and I think my heart is in the right place. But I'm not the only one who does it. A lot of people do it.

And a lot of people do do it. They realize, as Hugh Segal said, that there is a responsibility:

> We all have responsibilities to those who are disadvantaged, to those who share our society with us. We can't build a society based on a "winner-take-all" philosophy. The notion of selfishness as a kind of liberating force in our society isn't "on," and I don't think it's the Canadian way.

Media mogul Izzy Asper, founder and executive chair of CanWest Global Communications Corp., has contributed to many worthy causes in his hometown of Winnipeg, including a Jewish community centre and the university business school. In fact, in just one month, he signed three separate cheques for $10 million each. Said Asper:

> People have always thought of entrepreneurship as being risk and reward. That's not enough. In a country like this, the entrepreneur is someone who should risk, get reward and then show responsibility. That's pivotal and I have believed this all my life—I was taught this by my father. I come from

You have to give back. What you take out of life, you have to put back and help somebody else. Sometimes it's just somebody who is unhappy that you can make laugh a little bit.
MAUREEN FORRESTER, OPERA SINGER

immigrants who were so grateful to be allowed into this country that they drummed this into their children: You owe, you owe, you owe and you be a good citizen. And so I tried to pass that on to my children. Now, for me, it's payback time. I've done well. One of the largest beneficiaries of my work will be the public.

High-flying entrepreneur and visionary of the Virgin group of companies Sir Richard Branson also uses his wealth to good purpose:

> I think if you are a successful entrepreneur or businessman, you are no more successful than a successful broadcaster or a successful nurse, although great wealth comes with it—often the wealth of a small nation. So you have got to make sure that you use that wealth constructively, either using it to employ more people, setting up new companies, developing new products, competing with major corporations, campaigning on issues you feel strongly about, setting up charitable foundations. All of those things are important, not just because they're important, but they also make you feel good, make your staff feel good that they're not just working for a money-making machine, they're working for something they can feel proud of. I don't believe in personal indulgences. I believe that if you are wealthy, a certain responsibility comes with it.

It's what adults do, they take what they get and try and make something good out of it.

RICHARD FORD, AUTHOR

Bill Gates, the chair and chief software architect of Microsoft, and his wife, Melinda, have created many charitable foundations. They have funded many causes, from young high-tech entrepreneurs and Internet access in low-income communities to literacy and other educational programs, as well as research into AIDs, polio and vaccines:

> I enjoy trying to be as careful and thoughtful about giving the money away as I have been about creating Microsoft as a place where people thrive ... taking all that wealth and making sure it serves society's needs.

When singing sensation Shania Twain was growing up in Timmins, Ontario, there were days when she had no lunch to take to school, and now she's one of the wealthiest women in the entertainment business. More than anything, she told me, she's happiest about being able to make a difference:

Lend a helping hand, not necessarily charity, but some people need to be pulled up a little bit.

VINCE GILL, SINGER

> The most rewarding thing about being in the position I'm in is to be able to give back. I always wanted to be able to do that from my youth. I always promised myself that when I—and it was always "when"—when I make it someday, I am going to help kids that are in my position because it's no good to go to school without a lunch, not to have breakfast, to come home and there's no supper ready and there's nothing to cook supper with.

＠～

Being your brother's keeper is, as so many have said, its own reward. For those with wealth, it's a little easier to make a contribution. All of us, however, wealthy or not, have choices to make about how we act and how we react to each other and to the responsibilities we face. Taking responsibility is a recurring theme in almost every conversation I have had with almost anyone from almost any walk of life. I suppose I reflect my own biases and curiosities in the questions I pose, but for the most part, those who have become successful human beings raise the topic—willingly and unprompted. I have never, though, heard it so simply put as when Deepak Chopra leaned across my desk and, helpfully, parsed the word. "Response. Ability. Responsibility," he explained, "is your ability to respond creatively in challenging situations."

And the secret is, first, to take responsibility for yourself, and that often means just growing up. According to Dr. David Leibow, a psychiatrist and the author of *Love, Pain and the Whole Damn Thing*, becoming an adult is the collision course between unrealistic dreams and reality.

> There are several core traits to being an adult. One is taking responsibility for yourself—and I don't just mean being self-sufficient and independent but also autonomous in your thinking.

Gail Sheehy expressed it similarly:

If you are interested in your own destiny, you can have perhaps more choices available to you when you take on the responsibility.
LOREENA MCKENNITT,
SINGER AND SONGWRITER

You have to look after yourself … You are alone. There is no one who will always take care of you. When you realize that—because of a brush with your own mortality or a crisis of some proportion in our work or personal lives—that is really the significant move into adulthood.

John Le Carré could have—as so many seem to do—blamed his failures and disappointments in life on his childhood:

> I only had one parent because my mother disappeared when I was very young, so everything I knew about life, everything I trusted about life, was invested in my father. And my father was a monstrous—in the sense of looming very large—figure.

We have to take charge of our own lives … we are not made more successful by a magic wand waving …
MAEVE BINCHY, AUTHOR

As I set about doing my homework, I discovered that his father had been a charming con man and a very unreliable parent, and their complicated relationship had greatly influenced Le Carré's writing. "The older we get," Le Carré said, "the more interested we become in who we were, what we got from each parent." I had been over the moon when Le Carré agreed to be a guest because he so seldom grants interviews. I was also a fan, having read most of his eighteen bestsellers. But what was surprising and instructive was hearing how he had finally dealt with what he described as "a completely chaotic childhood." He came to believe that—no matter what—you are accountable for your own actions:

If you are a grownup, at a certain time, youth ceases to be an alibi. The excuses don't wash indefinitely. At a certain point, you say, "Stand up"—you're accountable for your own personality.

When I met actor Martin Sheen it was on the set of the wildly popular TV series *The West Wing*. Sheen plays the part of the U.S. president, and the Hollywood set, including the Oval Office, was so realistic that I began to believe he was. I wasn't alone. According to some pre-election polls, the fictional President Jed Bartlett would have won in a landslide had his name been on the ballot. As an outspoken and oft-jailed activist, Sheen loves the role and the show's underlying message: Democracy is about people—each of us—taking personal responsibility:

> When we watch Superman, don't we wish we had someone who could fly in and solve all our problems? It doesn't work that way. You and I have to do the work. You can't count on the government to save you from disaster. Democracy is about the people—the involvement of the people—who send extraordinary public servants to high office to serve the people, to serve high ideals—leadership.

Gloria Steinem had made a similar argument:

> I think that we cannot demand that our leaders be better than we are. We have to stop talking about them and talk about us.

The tragedy of ourselves is not the fault of the stars or in our leaders. Maybe it is in ourselves, maybe the dream is not there.

SENATOR LAURIER LAPIERRE

We are responsible for what it is within our power to change. So the question is not, What is somebody in power going to do?, but What are we going to make them do that needs doing?

Roberta Bondar, doctor, pilot, scientist, astronaut and, more recently, photographer of our national parks, has had her fair share of dealing with officialdom:

> Politicians have four-year attention spans, that's the way they are as a life form. But there has to be something that we, as individuals, want to put into a system that goes far beyond that—an ethic.

Empower yourselves as individuals and leaders to get involved, to organize yourselves, and recognize what you can do, then go out and do it.

TOM JACKSON, MUSICIAN

Laurier LaPierre has been on all sides of this debate as, at varying times, a journalist, author, broadcaster, civil servant and now senator. Whenever he's a guest on the program, the e-mail and letters pour in asking that Laurier run for office. Folks just react this way to the outspoken and passionate Quebecker, even when he chides us—as citizens—to take a hard look in the mirror:

> The energy we spend in criticizing the people we have elected, it is as if they had come down from some spaceship and nobody had ever heard of them before. We elected these people, we have to live with them. They are a reflection of ourselves. We have to assume the responsibility of who we are and act accordingly.

Laurier's comments really struck a chord. If "they" are a reflection of "us," then perhaps we ought to look a little more closely at what we have become. Mark Kingwell spent a lot of time thinking about this while writing *The World We Want*. He offered this challenging view of citizenship during our conservation:

> People now think of themselves primarily as consumers, or as householders, or as people who trade taxes for social programs, and they don't see that civic belonging might be a deeper sense of identity as it has been in the past. I'm not interested in turning the clock back, but in the past we understood citizenship based on various things—bloodlines, religious belief, constitutional belonging, ideology. But we're getting to a point where none of those answers is good enough in the world we are creating now, so we have to start thinking about citizenship as the act of participation itself. To be engaged in this action. Unless we get that sense of participatory citizenship alive in our minds, we're going to let things happen to us that I think we're going to regret very much later.

So can one person—the seemingly powerless individual—change the world by becoming engaged and taking responsibility or participating in some small way?

Violin virtuoso Isaac Stern is a gentle soul. I was almost afraid to shake his hand—if I squeezed too hard, I might deny the world the pleasure of his beautiful music. He smiled at my naïve concern as we began our conversation about music, but he was a chord away from his real message, about personal responsibility:

> I don't think it's enough for you and me to sit here and say, "Isn't it too bad?" You have to take individual action, and I can think of no greater responsibility than to see to the education of the young so they become civil and civilized members of a society. There is something to be learned about the beautiful part of life and what man's mind can create, and I think that that has a chance to make any child civilized.

Jane Goodall also made a compelling case for the fact that one can make a difference:

> Look at the world's problems and figure out where you can fix something—for the environment, for animals, for people and the community—figure out what can you do, what the problems are and which ones would you like to try to do something about. And always learn about it first, always look at it from the other side so when you end up having confrontations with people, you'll know why they are thinking the way they do.

Others echoed the need for citizens to look at all sides of the issues and to play by rules that are civil and fair so you leave others some ground to stand on. Michael Adams has written extensively on civic attitudes and behaviour:

I believe the system has to respect the individual, provide the individual with as much freedom and as much responsibility as possible.
P.J. O'ROURKE,
POLITICAL SATIRIST

Being a citizen means constructive engagement. It's confronting the other but not trying to establish a moral superiority that allows you later to blow them away.

Jason Sniderman is the son of an icon of the music business in Canada—Sam the Record Man. Sam taught his son an important lesson in civility in dealing with people in business, and in life:

I'm not a lefty. I'm a Red Tory. I believe in manners.
<small>Margaret Atwood,</small>
<small>author</small>

> The best lesson he taught me was never to push someone too far. At the end of the day, you have to leave something on the table for the other guy.

Dr. Henry Kissinger is the ultimate political operative and long-time diplomat. He agrees that the most important thing in an argument, next to being right, is to leave an escape hatch for your opponent so that he can gracefully swing over to your side without too much apparent loss of face:

> In diplomacy, you don't want total victory, because you have to keep dealing with these people again and again, and so your opposite, your counterpart, should feel that he achieved something as well.

In international diplomacy and in everyday life, respectful behaviour toward others is a prerequisite to a functional community. The Right Reverend Bill Phipps explained how challenging that can be:

One minute I'm sitting in hard-nosed political organizing meetings. Then, on behalf of the church, I go to the hospital to sit and hold a woman's hand whose child was dying. To me, God is in both those places. I might have been organizing against the racist, but then the family I would be sitting with at the hospital might be racist. It's irrelevant. You've got to be able to take their hand too. That's one of the things I firmly believe. You and I might disagree. You might be the enemy and I have to take you on in no uncertain terms and we should be able to go at each other, but as human beings, both of us are very fragile, vulnerable people and we're broken in many, many ways. It doesn't matter how success- ful or unsuccessful you or I are, we're human beings. And that's the fundamental thing.

∽∾

Regardless of the stated topic, many of my conversations eventually turn to the topic of civil behaviour. There's a real concern that basic common decency is disappearing. The experts call it "hit and run rudeness." The crux of the debate is whether people are simply rude and mannerless or whether their behaviour is indicative of a larger problem of society becoming less tolerant and compassionate. Perhaps the former is a reflection of the latter. Mark Kingwell expressed the fear that we're moving toward what he called the "torque" theory of life, which is that everything is either a claim or a liability, so we're always either avoiding risk or claiming that we've been done in by somebody else. "It's becoming a kind of litigious way of constructing our sense of each other," he told me, "and that's a very dangerous thing."

Mark shared a belief I've long held, that in smaller communities, civility is a crucial part of the social contract we have with one another. When you live in a small town and you deal with the same people on an ongoing basis, it's wiser to be respectful and pleasant. In contrast, within the anonymity of the city, rudeness or lack of civility has fewer—if any—immediate consequences. Those you bump into on the streets you're not likely to see again. But that is precisely why our obligations to the stranger should run deeper, because with the stranger we have no fear of reprisal, so it's a truer test of our behaviour and character. Mark fears, though, that in the new rude society we are too often rewarded for impoliteness, and the consequences are more far-reaching than we may realize:

> The problem is that it chips away at some kind of texture of obligation to other people and a sense that we're engaged in a common project. When everybody is just looking out for him- or herself, that really tears our sense of community apart.

Mark has a wonderful turn of phrase and this one bears repeating: "Manners and politeness are just the frozen surface of a deep lake of obligation." Or, as socially conscious business tycoon Richard Branson put it: "If you've dealt badly with people, you aren't going to sleep well, so it's better to deal well with people."

I think we're losing some of the nicer things in life. I think the manners of younger people are just atrocious.

Juliette, singer

Chapter Four

Becoming a Smarter Thinker

If you look at the three most important things in life, it's like a triangle: the top is values—personal values, spiritual values, religious values; then you have health; the third is thinking. People spend a lot of time on health, but how often do you hear someone say, "I'm interested in becoming a better thinker"?

DR. EDWARD DE BONO, AUTHOR

Thinking smarter is really about thinking in a different way. This idea has captivated me for years. So I've put these questions, time and again, to artists, Nobel laureates, high-tech gurus and to the world's leading thinker on thinking: How do we think? What's the difference between mind and brain?

Dr. de Bono has written more than sixty books. He teaches "thinking" to Nobel Prize winners and lectures in fifty-four countries. He also discovered and named the concept of lateral thinking, which he explains this way: "You can't dig a hole in a different place by digging the same hole deeper." Dr. de Bono somehow manages to make becoming a smarter thinker seem simple:

It's like a car: you can have a powerful engine, good suspension—that's the potential of the car. An intelligent brain also has a lot of potential—the neurons work faster. But the way you drive the car makes all the difference. So does the way you use your brain—and that's the thinking skill.

Dr. de Bono's brain is a marvel to watch. If only we could bottle it, I thought. In fact, another intriguing guest suggested that may soon be possible. Ray Kurzweil is a futurist, high-tech wizard and author of *The Age of Spiritual Machines: When Computers Exceed Human Intelligence*. As we sat in the studio, he matter-of-factly stated we are not far from the day when we will be able to download our brains onto computer disks. This led to a whole range of questions, including the big one: If we can download our intelligence, emotions, feelings and other thoughts into the computer, will we truly become immortal? People like Dr. de Bono and Ray Kurzweil do think differently. Kurzweil, for example, says the human emotion—not IQ—may be a more significant factor in solving difficult problems than we ever thought:

> Our emotion is actually the most complex, deep, rich, subtle thing that we do. It's the most intelligent thing we do, it's not some sort of byproduct or distraction from our intelligence. And it's the hardest thing for machines to emulate.

Daniel Goleman, a psychologist and former journalist, told me he was as shocked as anyone when his book about this idea, *Emotional Intelligence*, became a bestseller:

Emotional intelligence is really a different way of being smart. It's how you manage yourself and how you handle relationships. It involves self-awareness, managing emotions, motivation, empathy, social skills; those are not things you learn in school, those are abilities you learn in life.

So if being smart is about understanding people, human interaction and the human condition, and not just about ability to pass a test, memorize facts and retain data, then perhaps that explains why Goleman's book struck such a chord.

Barbra Streisand doesn't sing from her IQ. She sings from her soul.

DIANE DUPUY, FOUNDER, FAMOUS PEOPLE PLAYERS

It seems so self-evident when you say it—that how you deal with people is sometimes more important than how smart you are—but if you think about it, school is set up as though all that mattered was IQ, when, in fact, if you track people through their lives and look at how well you do in your marriage, as a parent, in the workplace, it depends much more on your emotional intelligence. IQ might get you hired, but EQ will get you promoted. There are studies that companies have done to see what makes someone outstanding as opposed to mediocre. They found that for jobs of all kinds, emotional intelligence abilities were twice as important as IQ and technical skill combined in distinguishing the stars from the average. The higher you go in the organization, the more it matters. For top leaders, it's eighty-five percent of the ingredients of star performance.

Fellow journalist Ann Medina, who has travelled the world and interviewed many people, was adamant about there being more to smartness than IQ:

> Brilliance is the most overrated virtue. How many times have we heard, "Oh, he's brilliant" or "She's brilliant," and sometimes they haven't got a soul in them and sometimes they're not smart.

That very point had come up in my earlier discussion with Dr. de Bono. Intelligent people, he said, aren't necessarily smarter; some highly intelligent people are poor thinkers because they can't think new thoughts.

> They take a view on a subject and use their thinking just to defend their point of view well, but they never see any need to listen to anyone else or to think of alternatives. So, a lot of intelligent people get trapped in poor ideas, because if you can defend a point of view well, you never see any need to listen to anyone else or to think of alternatives.

Not surprisingly, this led to a discussion about politics, and again Dr. de Bono agreed there was a need for some new thinking:

> The notion that one party has all the wisdom and the other is filled with idiots is so childish. Increasingly, the public is going

to put much more pressure on being constructive and not on how good you are at saying the other guys are idiots, and then things will change.

⮑⮐

I was looking forward to my conversation with the controversial power broker Dr. Henry Kissinger. Whether you like him or not, there is no doubting the man's genius, or his concern that, increasingly, experience and a sense of history don't count for much in the age of live, twenty-four-hour news:

> We have broadened our knowledge, but we have shortened our perspective.

I always have taught my children to consider the source.
ANNA QUINDLEN, AUTHOR

Kissinger is also troubled by how technology is changing political thinking. In his trademark hushed, conspiratorial tone that makes you strain to listen, Kissinger declared there's been a sea change in politics:

> Slogans have become more important than substance. People used to ask me what to think. Now they ask me what to say. It's a different attitude.

Dr. de Bono offered this assessment of our new reality:

> We have a system of thinking that is fine in a stable world, meaning the future is like the past. But when we've got

change, thinking in the past is an inadequate way to describe the future.

And that's exactly the concern that sparked an invitation to Dr. Thomas Homer-Dixon, professor, thinker and author of *The Ingenuity Gap: How Can We Solve the Problems of the Future?* He explores, through anecdote and powerful argument, the need for some radical new thinking to enable us to persist and survive. For example, the hammering of the environment that the lifestyle of the developed world imposes will not be solved by more money or technology. In our conversation, he made the point vividly. "Did you know," he asked, "that the largest man-made project in the world is not the Great Wall or the Pyramids but rather a garbage dump on Staten Island that covers an area of nine square kilometres?" He continued:

I'm not predicting anything. I just want you to watch CNN through a different lens.

WILLIAM GIBSON, AUTHOR

> The problems are getting harder—more complex—and at the same time, things are happening faster and so we need to supply the ideas faster. My argument is that sometimes the supply of ingenuity doesn't keep up with the rising requirement—that we can't solve our problems fast enough. Normally, we just think about running faster and faster, delivering more technologies and better and more complicated institutions and markets. But part of it is to think seriously about slowing the world down a bit and trying to reduce this relentless pace at which we make the world more complex and faster. At the moment, it's as if we've got the accelerator nailed to the floor.

The problem, Homer-Dixon explained, is that humans always seem able to adjust to dirty air, crowded streets, disease, poverty, war or stress. We walk past lakes or rivers that are too polluted for even a dog to brave. And while bottled water has become a trendy fashion accessory, we also have come to complacently accept it as a necessary reality. Such "adjusting" leads us to exploit the future, without considering the consequences. That's the crucial "gap" in our thinking. And despite our big brains, we're having trouble bridging the gap.

Stephen Jay Gould, an eminent paleontologist and evolutionary biologist at Harvard University, shares this concern:

> Evolutionists usually think of "success" in terms of persistence. And it's not clear that our big brains are conferring much persistence upon us. In fact, we are just as likely to blow ourselves up or poison our earth by virtue of this instrument in our head. The creatures who live for a long time—the real success stories—are bacteria, not people.

Edward O. Wilson, the renowned entomologist, is considered one of the world's greatest living scientists. He's also the Pulitzer Prize–winning author of *Concilience*, as well as many other books. "All we need to know is how to improve one organ," he said, tapping himself on the head. He continued:

> Intelligence means what you can learn. We are really the first species ever able to self-examine, think into the future and take control of ourselves and our environment.

If you want to understand the world and us, you have to understand the big picture. And I've never found a limit to it.

TIMOTHY FERRIS,
SCIENCE JOURNALIST

Homer-Dixon's hope is that the unique human capacity for metaphor —our ability to see patterns in vastly different things and have an emotional response to these patterns—will provide the ingenuity we need. So far, brains, technology or even self-interest have obviously not been enough. We may need to throw out some old ways of thinking. And despite our reverence for consistency, the smart mind often does house conflicting views. At the very least, as the cliché goes, the surest indication of a mediocre mind is the belief that everything can be explained. We haven't figured out all the questions yet, never mind the answers.

Dr. John Polanyi won the Nobel Prize in 1986, thirty years after his key discoveries in chemistry. He talked about the need to look at problems differently:

> There are contexts in which two and two is not equal to four. Everything needs examining and reexamining. Moving over here and taking a look from a new angle and seeing something that hasn't been seen before—those are the moments that really matter.

But those moments are not always recognized or accepted. In 1997, when I was invited to attend the Nobel Prize lectures and ceremonies in Stockholm, Sweden, I discovered that new thinking is often shunned before it's accepted and rewarded. This was my first visit to the homeland of my ancestors, and I found it very familiar, very Canadian—except, of course, for the darkness. December means that

Out of personal intellectual greed, I love to know the answers.

<small>TIMOTHY FERRIS, SCIENCE JOURNALIST</small>

there are only a few precious hours of daylight. The event, however, was enlightening. Dr. Stanley Prusiner had spent a lifetime trying to convince colleagues there was a third way—beyond germs and viruses—to transmit disease. And this form, which he called a prion, was, he believed, the culprit in mad cow disease. He had been dismissed as a heretic by many in his profession, but revenge was sweet as the most prestigious honour in the world was bestowed. When I finally had a chance to interview him several years later, we talked about the difficulty of a life of discovery and whether he believed he was a smarter thinker.

> I don't have an exceptional mind … if I had been more creative and more intelligent, I would have found another problem that was easier, but since I wasn't creative enough, I just hung in there because I wanted an answer.

Well, the world is glad he persevered, but for many there is neither time nor money to pursue that new idea, unless, of course, you're the richest man in the world. Bill Gates does what he calls "think weeks" several times a year just to boost his creativity and to "catch up." He told me this: "I don't think the way we think is changing, but I think that we have a lot more ability to find things that engage us." His advice is to surround yourself with thinking people:

> My motivation was always about building a cool product, working with smart people, solving the tough problems and

then going out and seeing how people are using it—what are they like, what would they like to have us make better, and so we have a lot left to do.

Betting on smart people and knowing that creativity is collaborative was also the advice of G. Scott Paterson, who made his first million when he was barely old enough to shave:

> A lot of it is gut instinct. I spend a lot of time with kids who come out of MBA schools and tell them, "You know, this is not a science. You've learned a lot of skills, but really, this is an art and at the end of the day it is the people." I am the kind of manager that would bet on a smart manager and a bad product rather than a good product and a bad manager any day of the week.

The phenomenal composer Marvin Hamlisch expressed a similar sentiment:

> I always feel that if I'm the stupidest person at the table, amongst the creators, I'm very happy. Give me creators who are really brilliant, and they bring me up.

Everyone was just a little intimidated as Hamlisch made his way into the studio for a rehearsal on the rented piano. Many a lesser talent had fussed and fumed about the less than perfect conditions for performing, the substandard equipment and the darkened studio laced with dozens of potentially lethal cables. But with a broad smile, he charged onto the set, slid onto the piano bench, hit three key chords and pronounced that everything was "just fine." Then, something almost unheard of with such stars, he thanked everyone for their time and trouble. Ten, maybe twenty seconds, start to finish. Watching the way his mind—and hands—worked was mesmerizing. Knowing that he had a heart was reassuring:

If you are ready to pay attention to something, you are much more likely to find it wonderful.
WALLACE SHAWN, PLAYWRIGHT AND ACTOR

> If you get complacent, then you're not going up on the ladder. I don't mean the ladder of success—I mean the ladder of creative achievement. My ego works this way and I hear it in my father's voice: "You know, Marvin, God blessed you. He gave you this gift. Now what you do with it is up to you."

Well, in the course of our interview Hamlisch put his gift to good use. In exchange for his heart's desire—a simple tuna sandwich from the cafeteria—he composed a whole new theme song for our program right on the spot, no charge.

You don't have to win a Nobel Prize or have a room full of Grammys to be creative. A simple act of kindness or even a great meal are also creative acts. "Food, perfectly conceived, is beautiful and worth crying over," said Julia Child, the grande dame of the culinary world. Thinking smarter—more creatively—requires using both sides of the brain, according to Child:

If you have the recipe in your head and can improvise, then you're a real cook. Creativity with no practical knowledge doesn't work.

When we use a word like "creative" we tend to think of the true artists—the painter, the songwriter, the novelist—who often react to life with their emotional intelligence.

⌒⌒

People think of fiction writers as intellects. They're not. It is not a highly intellectual activity. I take little bits and pieces of the cloth rag from the rag bin in my own mind and sew them together. E.L. DOCTOROW, AUTHOR

I've never spent more than an hour and a half writing one song. I think the muses visit you from time to time—you have to realize when that's happening, work with the moment, capture the moment, get the machines running, get it on tape and move on. BURTON CUMMINGS, SINGER AND SONGWRITER

⌒⌒

If it's not the muses, perhaps it's just the luck of the gods that makes us become smarter thinkers, at least according to the late Dr. Michael Smith, Canada's most distinguished biochemist and genetic researcher, and winner of a Nobel Prize in 1993:

I'm not that smart ... but there are a few things I'm good at. I was good at chemistry and physics and math and hopeless at literature and language—it's just an accident of the miracle of what our individual brains are.

Dr. Tak Mak, who discovered the key to the immune system, offered this comment:

You can't really say that the smartest person is going to do the best. Sometimes it's a matter of how you take advantage of your luck.

Despite the eloquence of all these great minds, it is still from the mouths of babes that genius often flows. And one of the smartest people I've ever met was five at the time. Musical prodigy Wesley Chu was writing his own compositions and performing on public stages when he still needed a booster seat on the piano bench. He has an IQ of 165 and loves to play the piano. When I asked him how he memorizes all the songs and music he performs, Wesley answered:

I don't memorize. I put it in my heart, and when I need it, I just open up my heart.

Chapter Five

Staying Stupid

*Sometimes the most amazing things happen to you if you have
the right mental attitude.*
AL PURDY, POET

A few years ago, amid the daily batch of snail mail from viewers, I received a letter whose author told me that I "had the best job—except for that of tenor or poet." The letter was signed "Al Purdy." A few weeks later, another envelope from one of Canada's greatest wordsmiths (he published more than forty volumes of poetry) arrived, and this time he had enclosed a poem titled "A Handful of Earth for René Lévesque." I was flattered and intrigued by these poetic missives, and so when Purdy next travelled from the west coast to Toronto, I invited him to come by for a long chat.

As he sat across from me in the studio, he was awkward in his chair, fidgety, and uncertain as to why he had agreed to the evening. When I tried to introduce him as one of Canada's finest living poets, he barked, "Stop calling me that … it's like being a braggart." He went on to make his case, describing himself instead as "a high school dropout, a bankrupt businessman, an inconsiderate son, a problem husband and a demoted soldier." In fact, he was demoted so many times while in the armed forces, he said, that finally he was saluting civilians.

He'd made a joke, found his comfort zone, and I could see him thinking, *Okay, I'm in control. I've set the stage.* Then he smiled and announced, "Every single word I say is a lie." In the course of our conversation he revealed that he had a wonderful, though sometimes bizarre, sense of humour. And then, as often happens in these encounters, there was a moment of truth. It slipped unsuspectingly through his lips when Purdy declared his personal mantra to be "Stay stupid," a phrase borrowed from an Australian poet, which, said Purdy, meant "Keep your mind open." Poets are observers who see with their eyes and their heart, and Purdy's willingness to see new things is what kept his brain so active and creative for so long.

Someone asked me recently what part of my brain or my mind was the key to the ability to prepare and conduct so many interviews on such a vast array of topics. "Curiosity," I answered, without hesitation. That is what keeps the mind open. Teachers and parents are crucial as it is they who instill or squelch that early curiosity and willingness to stay stupid while becoming smart.

Joni Mitchell is considered the single most influential woman in pop music—a fine musician and a poetic lyricist with a velvety voice deepened by time and smoke. When I talked with the living legend—poolside in Los Angeles—she gave credit to one potent mentor:

A lot of my life is ignorance of how to proceed.

FRANK McCOURT, PULITZER PRIZE–WINNING AUTHOR

I had an extraordinary teacher—a maker of writers and a maker of athletes and a stirrer up of spirit. He knew how to make you wild and put the lid on you. He told me to "write in my own blood." He told me this at the age of eleven.

And so she did. She opened up her mind to see what was there. "What things are you going to write about?" she asked. "Things that are on your mind or on your heart."

Physical surroundings can also stir the soul and expand horizons. Mitchell, the songstress of Saskatchewan, believes small towns and miles of prairie ignited her curiosity about the world:

> Every morning the train would blow its whistle as it entered the bend before the town of Maidstone ... We lived out on the highway. Traffic then was pretty sparse, but the train came every day, and there were buses going by and the occasional car. But the coming and going of things—to sit next to that hard ocean, so to speak, and see things coming and going— inflamed my curiosity as a child. "Where are they going?" And so I used to hear the whistle blow at the curve and run to the window, see that puff of smoke, and I'd wave at the conductor.

Ann-Marie MacDonald's sweeping family epic *Fall on Your Knees* wowed the critics and captured the minds of millions of readers. She explained how keeping her mind open allowed her to discover the story she wanted to tell:

I used to know a lot about writing, and now I don't. I don't know anything.

E.L. DOCTOROW, AUTHOR

I wanted to free up my unconscious. I wanted to go psychically naked into the wilderness of stories and see what would ambush me.

We hear the buzz phrase "lifelong learning" in many contexts these days. Art Garfunkel, the voice of a generation, gave it real meaning. Later in life he went back and began to reread everything he'd read and been taught in university:

That's good stuff, that Tolstoy, and you want to know what Thomas Hobbes was really saying. It turns out there is a reason why any good university will say, "These are the things we think you should know about," and the idea that they pass through our twenty-one-year-old minds and that's not good enough. They are too weighty and too thought-provoking for us to not slow down later on and check it out. So read Freud and Karl Marx in your thirties.

The artist Ken Danby has broad shoulders and movie-star good looks. He plays hockey and is every bit a man's man. His powerful hands belie his gentle artist's touch, and his sparkling eyes are a window on a mind that sees reality in sharp relief. Ken is one of the world's best-known realists, painting his first award-winning picture—a portrait of his dad—when he was ten. Ken was eventually warned that if he was going to make a mark, he'd have to hop on the artistic bandwagon of the day, which happened to be abstract expressionism. But sometimes, Ken told me, you have to go backward to go forward:

I see life as one long university education that I never had.
SIR RICHARD BRANSON,
ENTREPRENEUR

I tried it and I felt capable of doing these things, but they didn't really sustain my interest. I went back to the original challenges I grew up with—a representational direction of painting—and time has proven that we've come back to it.

He told me the story of taking his famous painting *At the Crease* to be part of a gallery show back in 1972. The dealer took a look and declared, "Who would want this? What should we do with it?" Fortunately, the buying public had an open mind and embraced the young artist's work.

I've never had any kind of strategy for a career. I've just done what seemed interesting at the time.
PAUL GROSS, ACTOR

Ken always keeps his mind open. "Embrace all directions that have merit and achieve some balance" is his mantra. And then he added perhaps his most passionate point:

> You can be multitalented, you can be gifted, you can have the facility, you can have all the control and have all the hand-eye coordination and whatever … there's one thing missing that will make the difference, and that is desire. Desire is everything. Talent is nothing. Desire is paramount in anything you do, really.

Loreena McKennitt was a young girl from Morden, Manitoba, who wanted to be a veterinarian. But before long she was busking on the streets and on her way to international acclaim as a singer and songwriter. Loreena didn't set out to become a star, she explained, she just followed her instinct to express herself through words and music. Though her success—she is self-managed, self-produced and head of her own record label—has required hard work and strategic thinking about how to create the right situations, Loreena says you sometimes don't know—and aren't supposed to know—where life will take you:

> I am preparing myself for things that I don't know if and when they will happen ... "A good traveller has no fixed plans and is not intent on arriving" is a phrase that reflects my whole life in a way.

Life is to get out there and be learned—I want to react to life still and I want to see what's waiting for me tomorrow. I don't want to know.

VINCE GILL, SINGER

I knew exactly what she meant the moment she said it. No *fixed* plans does not mean no plans. It just means there may be different schedules and many routes to the same place. It's about staying open to unexpected possibilities, reaching out into the unknowable and genuinely being willing to embrace whatever comes. This is much the way I've lived my own life, and countless others have expressed the same idea. You don't want to become too attached to a specific goal, because you might miss a life-altering opportunity. Singer Helen Reddy, the voice of the song "I Am Woman," that stirred a generation, said this:

> Where will I be this time next year and what will I be doing? I have no idea, and that's one of the things I really like about my life.

Chapter Six

Doing Your Homework

People believe in this crap about inspiration. They say it bubbles up like nightingale song. It don't. I am at my desk every morning at nine or nine-thirty till four o'clock, every day, every week, every month, and this has been going on for forty years. Hard work? It's like crawling the distance of a football field on your bare hands and knees, and it ain't Astroturf, kid, it's carpeted with broken glass.
W.O. MITCHELL, AUTHOR

The weather was dismal, I was pressed for time, but I would have walked from Toronto to Calgary for a chance to talk with the gruff but lovable man who had written the ultimate story of the Prairies, *Who Has Seen the Wind*. Wiser heads prevailed and I took a plane, with a red-eye return late that night. When W.O. didn't answer the door because he was squeezing in a nap before our conversation, there was a series of panic calls and a mini crisis or two, but before long we were inside, where the writer and Merna, his companion for life, editor and wife (she was all three), welcomed us.

As we set up the cameras, she issued some final instructions—not to us, but to him. No chewing tobacco, she said, and no spitting, although there were already plenty of telltale signs of the black juice down the front of his red turtleneck. And try, she said in what she thought was a more realistic command, to keep the swearing under control. And try he did when I asked him which of his own books was his favourite. "The best you have done to date is the one you're working on—and if you're not in the mood, you're going to fall on your—" As he searched for a more polite word than "ass," he finally smiled and shrugged. "Well," he remarked, "I said I'd keep it clean."

While many in the artistic community refer to their "talent" as a gift—arguing they are just a vehicle to transmit creative works—the most successful realize their talent, or genius, is a product of hard work. The great novel is not magically downloaded into a brain. And a performer must practise.

W.O. had that work ethic and would have loved the description of hard work offered up by rock legend Rompin' Ronnie Hawkins on our set one night:

> I've played in places where you had to show your razor and puke twice before they'd let you in.

Other performers, like Pinchas Zukerman, the violin virtuoso and conductor, put it more delicately:

> I've been doing this for a long time. You need to prepare for that journey. You need to fill that tank with a lot of information. Imagine how many times I've opened up the violin case in forty-three years.

Mr. Zukerman said discipline is needed to master an instrument or an art form—or for that matter, any other skill in life:

> Talent is not enough. Anyone who thinks that should quit. You've got to work very hard. The reason it looks easy is because of the hard work, which means most of the time we know what we're doing.

The soft-spoken country star Charlie Major wasn't always so quiet, but he did eventually learn the same lesson about hard work:

> Until I was about thirty years old, I spent a lot of time partying. I think everybody is born with talent, but it took me a longer time than others to realize that you have to actually work at it to further that talent. I tried to get by on my talent for a lot of years and I did—I made a living at it. But I woke up one day and realized "maybe if I work a little harder at it, I'll get somewhere."

The most difficult thing to do in writing is the discipline of doing it—but a dictionary comes in handy as well.
RODDY DOYLE, BOOKER PRIZE—WINNING AUTHOR

Ed Robertson of the Barenaked Ladies told me that the band's success has been the result of hard work and perseverance:

> Hard work is what did it. We just kept going back—three times a year to each place for four or five years. Thanks to our manager's "you must work all the time" policy, it finally paid off.

And there were other rewards for Robertson as well: "I am aware every second that I am on stage," he told me, "that I was a geek in high school and all those girls that are screaming now were not screaming for me then."

Wayne Gretzky says it was his father who explained the benefits—and there have been many—of working hard and working early:

> My father told me, "You know, the more you work now and don't play, when you get older the more you'll be able to play and the less work you'll have to do." It's true—the harder you work at sixteen, seventeen, eighteen, the more you're going to enjoy life when you are older.

Blues legend BB King made the interesting point that in most other professions, there is an acknowledgement of lifelong learning. We refer to practising doctors, practising lawyers, so why not practising musicians? "I work hard at auditioning ... every day," he explained. Well into his seventies, King is still doing a gruelling concert tour of 250 shows a year. There was a moment of sadness, though, as he added that even though he loves his work, the late nights and constant travel have meant that he's missed a lot of special moments in life—a son's graduation or a fellow musician's concert. As he and others know, hard work often does mean sacrifice.

George Chuvalo, the greatest fighter that Canada ever produced, held the Canadian heavyweight boxing championship for

I go and do my best. When I go to bed at night, I'll say, "Well, I did my best, not good enough, I'll try harder tomorrow."

SENATOR SISTER
PEGGY BUTTS

more than two decades and twice went the distance with Muhammad Ali, a feat that took both hard work and sacrifice.

> You have to be so disciplined. And it's not just what you have to do—it's what you have to do without.

George is a man who knows about loss. Not in the ring, but in life. He lost three sons and his wife to either drugs or suicide. Even in his times of grief, he has kept up a tiring speaking schedule, taking his antidrug message to kids.

For those who live and work in the public eye, there is always an expectation to be your best—regardless of circumstances—and to be willing to bare all, emotionally speaking. It brings to mind the words of actress Rosalind Russell, who said that acting is like standing up naked and turning around slowly.

Terry Evanshen knows how that feels. When he was forty-four years old, Evanshen, a member of the Canadian Football Hall of Fame and a Grey Cup champion, was in a devastating car accident. He was so close to death that last rites were administered. He lapsed into a coma and, when he woke up, suffered severe amnesia. His life was a blank slate.

> My wife is my childhood sweetheart. I didn't recognize her. I didn't know what a wife even was, as a concept.

He began slowly to reconstruct his own history so he could attempt to re-create the person he once was. He had to settle for creating a person, period.

> I don't have the Terry Evanshen of the past, so I had to start to build a new one. I didn't know right from wrong. I even had to learn to hug again—I didn't know what a hug was or why people did it.

Starting over from scratch, discovering your physicality and all of life's nuances, must be unimaginably frustrating. It is also awe-inspiring. Terry has become a motivational speaker because of his rare vantage point on what it means to give it your best:

> I'm standing naked on the stage. I can't fabricate a facade. I'm giving you one hundred percent. Look deep within yourselves. Are you really giving a hundred percent and being your best? No pretension here, because you're only hurting yourself if you aren't.

Comedian Frank Shuster and his partner Johnny Wayne appeared sixty-seven times—more than anyone else—on the *Ed Sullivan Show*, and every time it was live and unedited. Shuster recalled their performances:

> We had to go all out because we couldn't do it again. A director could say, "We can live with it," and we'd say, "Yeah, but

we'll die with it," if we knew it wasn't working. So we went all out—every time.

For politicians, performers or those of us who ply our trade on the TV screens of the nation, you must, as they say, put your best foot forward. I remember as a young and cocky TV journalist heading off to interview the then prime minister, Pierre Trudeau. This was shortly after the now famous "finger" to the folks in Salmon Arm, and his Liberal Party was sagging in the polls. This prompted me to declare that perhaps he had lost the moral authority to govern and should—obviously—step aside. A smug, condescending smile crept across his face as he began to dismiss my rather novel theory of democracy. He mockingly suggested that if I were right, then all he had to do—when he was back up in the polls—was merely suspend elections, dispense with all the cumbersome democratic machinery and declare himself prime minister for life. The civics lesson was mercifully short, but Trudeau had managed to both humiliate me on national television and instruct me in one of the most important journalistic lessons of my life: Never ask a question you don't know the answer to; do your homework and be prepared.

I remember saying to myself I'm going to be the next Margaret Laurence. Now, you can only think that when you're twenty.
GAIL ANDERSON-DARGATZ, AUTHOR

❧

I take notes. I keep a grocery list of the details I absorb. And other details I need to know. I travel with a notebook all the time. JOHN IRVING, NOVELIST

My whole life I've walked around with my business card in my pocket. GEORGE A. COHON, CEO OF MCDONALD'S CANADA

What you do with opportunity, maybe that's a talent. But it has to be understood that if you're going to survive in this world, you have to take advantage of your opportunities. TOM JACKSON, MUSICIAN

ᗌᗘ

Sir Richard Branson had a youthful experience of the necessity of being prepared. When he was just eight, his mother put him out of the car, blocks from home, and told him to make his own way. He was not being punished, he explained, he was being taught to use his own wits, to test his own memory and to learn how to cope with the unforeseen—to be prepared. It turned out that Branson needed a few more Boy Scout lessons. His mother eventually launched a search party to locate her lost son, but Branson has always been prepared, whatever the risk. "Life is full of risks. I like to push myself forward and challenge myself."

ᗌᗘ

Time and again in my conversations with the successful and talented, that message has been echoed. It doesn't matter if your talent is God-given or not, it does not magically unfold. Talent requires hard work, preparation and, as three-time world champion and two-time Olympic silver medallist skater Elvis Stojko explained, an ability to focus on the task at hand:

It's ninety percent a mental state. Your body will always follow the mind. Whatever the mind says, the body will follow. And if you keep saying it, the body will believe it. Your system will believe it. Your spirit will believe it.

For those whose bodies are their creative tool, the importance of mind over that fickle matter is decisive. Seldom do we out-of-shape normal mortals have to face those all-or-nothing, do-or-die moments—with success, gold, pride, millions of dollars in endorsements and the hopes of an entire nation dependent on whether you can land a quad followed by a triple Axel or shave a quarter-second from your stride. We have much to learn about attitude from professional athletes. Victory is decided by a split second, and years of hard work can be vanquished by a tiny misstep. Here's how Canadian sprinter Donovan Bailey, once the fastest man in the world and Olympic champion, deals with the pressure:

Practise every day. Don't skip days. Playing an instrument, you're not owed anything. It's about the work … You can't lose sight of your work ethic.
Wynton Marsalis, jazz musician

> I believe that when I am truly focused, when I'm focusing on accomplishing something, when I'm in my zone … no one can actually compete with me.

Athletes must also manage their time so that achieving perfection does not consume their life. As Donovan and I strolled—not sprinted—through a park in Austin, Texas, where he was training, he talked about the importance of having a life:

I am not just a runner. You know, track is track, and reality is reality. But I think I have the ability to balance both. I want to be successful in whatever I do while still maintaining and being the person that I am.

For athletes and actors, says Emmy and Tony Award–winning actor Joe Mantegna, it's the pressure of competition that often brings out the best:

> Just observe, if nothing else. You're going to pick up something from watching the best do what they do, and so, as an actor, that's what you hope to do. It's like running a race. You always find that records are usually broken in a race when runners are running against other world-class runners. They obviously have the capacity to run that speed whether they're running alone or not, but they're just pushed that extra bit when that guy next to you is almost as good as you are—or maybe even a little bit better … that just drives you that much harder.

Of course, setting your mind to the task at hand is hard to do— there are many distractions, many physical or psychological limitations on our abilities or mindset, and few of us could concentrate years of effort on a single event, like winning a race. Nor do we experience such intense and concentrated competition. In the artistic world there is, of course, competition, but not many set out to win the Pulitzer or the Oscar in the beginning. The important thing is to just set out.

All work, in its purest form, is an art. So in other words, if you apply yourself to be the best, you can do it. If it's done to the best of your ability and the best of your skill and focus and attention, then if somebody later wants to define it as art, then so be it. That's what I do. This is my job. JOE MANTEGNA, ACTOR

My aspirations were very modest. I used to think, "Oh, it would be wonderful to get one poem published"—or one story. I never thought I could write a whole book. But I found out—and every writer finds this out—you just do it one day at a time. You do it one page at a time. CAROL SHIELDS, PULITZER PRIZE–WINNING AUTHOR

You never know what's going to happen in your life—as long as you give it everything you have, and you really try hard and you're a good person, then who knows what's going to happen. KIM STOCKWOOD, SINGER

Damon Stoudamire was the shortest guy on the basketball court but a powerhouse for the Toronto Raptors. He had been recruited to play basketball by former star player and, at the time, Raptors vice president Isiah Thomas. Damon related the lesson he learned from Thomas:

The most important thing Isiah ever taught me was "to win and forget and to lose and forget. Don't get too high when you win and don't get too low when you lose … it's easy to lose and not easy to win."

As for all things in life, attitude and perspective are key. When sitting across the desk from the man whose team had been the first to scale Mount Everest, I was taken aback by Sir Edmund Hillary's view of what many would have deemed to be the ultimate success:

> When we reached the summit, one of the thoughts I had was that we'd really only done half the job—we still had to get to the bottom again.

Everyday life can often seem like tackling our own Mount Everest— our tasks are never done, the time is always too short. But if you do your homework and set out to perform your best, often a little bit of luck comes your way. Throughout my working years I have often had a sense of serendipity working its gentle magic. If I were set to talk with an important thinker, I would inevitably run across an obscure magazine or a book that shed light or offered a perspective. I remember once being in the car heading for the airport en route to Calgary to give a speech. I had been too busy to write it in advance, and the plane trip would be my only chance. The problem was that I did not have the right idea. Steve, the driver, casually handed me a copy of *Harper's* magazine, suggesting that there were several interesting arti-

In any situation and when we are at our best, there is that collision of real human drama and the absurd.

PAUL GROSS, ACTOR

cles I might want to read on the plane. I flipped through the pages—still quietly panicking over my ever-shrinking timetable—and a headline caught my attention. The article that followed triggered an idea that would become the core of my speech. It was one of life's serendipitous moments.

Science fiction visionary William Gibson defined serendipity this way:

> Over the years I seem to have become covered in some kind of invisible flypaper and, as I walk around, these ideas just stick. Then I pick them all off and make a book.

But it was a story that E.L. Doctorow told me that made me a believer in the serendipitous force:

> Somehow I figured this out early. What you do is, you start writing first and if you are writing well, whatever you need will come to hand. You build kind of a magnetic force field around you and whatever you need comes to hand—it kind of flies out of the air. I remember, in *Ragtime*, I decided to send the little girl on trolley cars from New York up to Lowell, Massachusetts. I wanted to get them there so they could participate in the great bread and roses textile strike. I knew there was an intricate system of trolley cars in those days, but I didn't know that it could actually be done. I wrote that you could pay a nickel and go to the end of the line and then wait

I feel very lucky to be at this point in my life and to be having this much fun and having this career with no end yet in sight. I think it's luck, it's hard work and it's talent, and you have to have all three—any combination of only two doesn't work.

JIMMY BUFFETT, MUSICIAN

for the next interurban trolley car and take it. But I didn't know if that was true or not, so I thought I'd better check it. I was wandering around the midtown branch of the New York Public Library and I happened to pass a shelf of oversized books that were protruding out from the shelf, and my elbow hit one of them and I picked it up and opened it and it was a history of trolley car companies in America. It told me everything I needed to know. I think these things happen when you're working. Whatever you need, you will find.

Chapter Seven

Playing the Cards
You're Dealt

My journey is an example of the kind of potential inside every person with a disability—if we remove the barriers that don't need to be there.
RICK HANSEN, ACTIVIST

The first time I met Rick Hansen was under the most unusual of circumstances. John Crosbie, the former Conservative finance minister, had volunteered to be "roasted" at a posh black-tie affair in the nation's capital. Anyone who was anyone in the political world was there. René Lévesque, the lovable little powerhouse who was the heart and soul of Quebec nationalism, and I were co-hosts of this gathering designed to raise funds for The Man in Motion world tour to benefit spinal cord injuries research. You could tell on first meeting him that there was something that set Rick Hansen apart—his intense eyes, the conviction in each sentence. That night, and in the course of several subsequent interviews, I was able to get inside that mind. He was a man who—because of his tragedy—had become a better and more interesting person. It was all part of the journey. Rick recalled how this marathon that would change the mindset of millions—not to mention his life—began with the foolish bravado of four guys who thought they'd get a motorhome and watch Rick wheel fifty miles a day in his wheelchair and that would be that:

> It's probably better that we were so naïve and had no idea what we were getting ourselves into. We were armed with a lot of courage, a lot of heart and not much know-how.

It's often just a fluke that some causes and characters capture the public's imagination and others do not. Terry Fox, the young man who'd lost a leg to cancer, embarked on an unlikely and highly risky mission to run across Canada to help raise money for cancer research. Terry touched the nation, and his was a tough act for anyone to follow. Charisma and character would be the minimum requirements. Rick Hansen had more than enough to spare. Using his wheelchair, he would circle the globe:

> Being a real close friend of Terry Fox—we played wheelchair basketball together—I watched his journey as he went across the country, I saw how he changed people's attitudes—people started to look at people with disabilities in a more positive light.

For months there was just pain, miles and miles of nothing but road and few people along the way to spur Rick on. "It really tested my motivation," he explained:

At the beginning, when the interest was so sporadic, I was so frustrated I didn't know if I could continue, and then I'd see one young man in a wheelchair. "Go for it, Rick!" he'd yell out. "If you can do that, I'm going to go to school and finish my graduate degree!" And I'd hang on to that memory for all it was worth because I didn't know when the next one would come.

Despite his almost miraculous accomplishment, Rick was and remains frustrated by the physical limitations:

> Sure, I have moments. Say I'm at home and want to move the television out of the way. I'm a husband and a father and I want to do those things. But I can't—I'm a strong guy but I can't use my back. So, that's really frustrating. I have a little pout and then I have to just get on with it—because there are lots of things that I can't do and if I focused on those things, I'd never be happy.

Still, I was stunned, though in the end not surprised, when I asked Rick if, given his life today, he would still climb into the back of that truck with the drunk driver at the wheel. His answer was an emphatic yes.

> As tragic and as challenging as it was, I was forced to dig deep, and I was able to live a quality of life that I don't think I ever would have had if I hadn't had that challenge. We're a combination of what we're born with, the things that happen to us, our environment and the choices we make. I wouldn't have

What faith is, to me, is simply saying that I am going to live, I'm going to take what comes next— even though I don't understand it.

THOMAS MOORE, AUTHOR

had the opportunity to find out who I was if that hadn't happened to me. And I wouldn't trade the experiences I've had—meeting my wife, Amanda, the children, the tour, the ability to contribute, the sense of meaning ... just for the use of my legs.

The strength of his character and the force of his will are powerful. This is the quality we all strive for—my grandmother used to call it backbone, and if you had it, you were worth listening to. I've had several encounters with Rick over the years, and he is always worth listening to:

> I choose not to be a victim because I know that things happen to me that I can't control. I know there are thousands of things I can't do—whether I have a disability or not. As a matter of fact, what is a disability? We all have disabilities so it's what we focus on, and I like to focus on the things I can do.

⌒⌒

The virtuoso violinist Itzhak Perlman contracted polio when he was just four. Now as then, he told me, there is a tendency for people to look at the disabled and think, "If they cannot walk, they can't do anything else." But his parents encouraged him to play his violin, pointing out that, after all, his hands were not affected. He recalled their advice:

> My parents said I had to realize what I could do and what I couldn't do. I couldn't walk any more without braces or

If I ask myself at the end of the day "What is true meaning?", am I going to measure it by the fact that I am able to walk around? I don't think so. That's not what you're thinking about.

RICK HANSEN, ACTIVIST

crutches, but nothing had changed in my ability to play. I had to separate my abilities from my disabilities.

⮑⮐

When Ian Scott first ran for political office, he promised to lose. He did. But eventually Ian went on to become the eloquent and dashing attorney general of Ontario. A powerful orator and a brilliant legal mind, he played a key role in everything from the Berger Commission to the Meech Lake debate. But in 1994, fate buried his former life beneath the rubble of a stroke. When I asked him to be a guest on our television program and engage in an hour-long conversation, he asked if I was crazy. Despite a large vocabulary, Ian speaks only in bursts of three or four words. A friend who accompanied him on the set explained that it's as if the computer is working but the printer has jammed. Now, usually, the best TV "guest" is articulate, or as we say in the business, a good talker. But, despite the abbreviated answers, Ian remains an effective communicator. He expressed his longing for the civility that once defined partisan exchange and that sadly, according to Ian, no longer does. He misses politics and the law. And there is a predictable frustration and anger over this loss of ability and function. Still, all but silenced by the stroke, Ian has been able to re-create a life in which conversation, debate and the exchange of ideas are possible. And he continues to be a passionate example of the triumph of hope and the power of the human spirit.

Dr. Robert Buckman is a renowned oncologist and broadcaster, author of ten books and a survivor of cancer. For him, it's mind over

I just don't accept no for an answer. Perseverance—being able to get up and dust yourself off and get it going again.
ED MCMAHON,
BROADCASTER

matter—how you look at a problem will dictate whether you triumph. He talked about what matters in life:

> Attitude is extremely important for living. But how you actually live your life becomes even more important when your quality of life is threatened, whether it's threatened by divorce or unemployment or bereavement or cancer. It's important to work out what really matters.

Michael Korda, editor in chief of Simon & Shuster for more than forty years, is the author of several bestselling books, including *Man to Man*, which is about surviving cancer. He has in his own words become a poster boy for prostate cancer:

> I had never had a serious illness and so it was extraordinarily difficult for me to conceive that I had cancer. When I was told I tested positive, I had to write on a yellow legal pad over and over again "I have cancer, I have cancer, I have cancer" before I could even say it. It was like a bolt of lightning.

He was a man about town, an influential force in the publishing world, but cancer does not discriminate—he had no choice but to play the cards he was dealt.

> I learned patience, because as a workaholic I was very active. But then I was forced to become dependent on other people

I've learned that a lot of life is awfully uncomfortable— even when you are as fortunate as I am. And, a lot of it is glorious. And into every life a little rain must fall.

HUME CRONYN, ACTOR

to look after me, and they were immensely patient with me. I learned from that the value of being patient—not only with other people, which is comparatively easy, but with myself, which is much harder. You do come to grips with mortality, and one of the things I brought away from the experience of cancer was the sense that if there was something I wanted to do, then by God I had better do it now and not wait. I don't like to put things off any more. You bring some good things away from the experience. If you don't die, then I think you can learn something from cancer.

What will be will be. My role today is just to live each day as it comes.

JEAN VANIER, HUMANITARIAN

Political columnist Allan Fotheringham also learned something from cancer. The man who has graced the back page of *Maclean's* magazine since dinosaurs roamed the earth found out he had prostate cancer just three weeks after his wedding:

A funny thing happened to me on the way to getting married. I had a prostate exam. I'd never been sick a day in my life. I didn't even know where my prostate was.

He too confronted his own mortality and learned to take life as it comes. He described the effect living with cancer had:

It makes you think a bit. Calms you down a bit. You think about what is really important in life, and the only thing is health.

The two commodities in life that you really cannot buy are health and time. MARVIN HAMLISCH, COMPOSER

Time should be lengthened by joy, by happiness, by who you're with, by the food you're eating and the times you're having.
GORDON PINSENT, ACTOR, DIRECTOR AND WRITER

Life is sweet, you know. I've never met a person who really wanted to die. We want to live.
DR. MARIUS BARNARD,
HEART SURGEON

Perhaps the most difficult person to interview is a friend. Scott Simmie had been a colleague and was a highly intelligent and wonderfully articulate journalist. Scott had been able to mask his symptoms because the TV news business creates and tolerates a lot of bizarre and unusual behaviour. But he suffered from and finally confronted his mental illness. This was not some anonymous "victim" or a statistic. With remarkable courage, he willingly shared the story of his encounter with madness, which he described as a "a fantastic and terrifying voyage through several countries and a number of states of mind."

Finally identified as suffering from bipolar affective disorder, Scott recounted his time as a foreign correspondent in Moscow, when the symptoms of his disease first began to present themselves—depression followed by manic sprees and then delusions of grandeur. He describes the hospitalization, the misdiagnoses that led to prescription drug overdoses, and the inevitable thoughts of suicide. It's an odyssey he's lucky to have survived.

Part of the inspiration for telling his story came from his journalistic instinct and a belief that there is—more often than we'd care to admit—no "us" and "them." While undergoing treatment in Toronto, Scott followed the case of Edmond Yu, a young paranoid schizophrenic who was shot and killed by Toronto police. Scott identified with Yu's bizarre behaviour, realizing how easily it could have been him and how unprepared we all are for recognizing and responding properly to mental illness:

> I think people don't know how to react. Mental illness just really does scare the hell out of you. I know certainly in the past, when I'd be walking down the street and I would see someone with sort of overt signs of mental illness, maybe babbling to themselves or whatever, I would make a U-turn and think to myself, "Yeesh, don't want to be anywhere near that person." But those people are people, and those people have families and those people deserve to be treated as such.

Scott says that the stigma of mental illness "can be more painful than the disorder itself." People lose their jobs, friends, family and the ability to control their lives: "In my own personal case, it was huge, it was monumental. I believe, in fact, it was the worst part of my illness."

That stigma cost Cameron Wilson, son of former finance minister Michael Wilson, his life. Suffering from debilitating depression, Cameron committed suicide. His father hopes his message will help others:

The reason why I speak out about it is because of Cameron, and I can see that some of the things that were bothering Cameron—who pleaded with us *not* to speak out about his illness—robbed him of some of that important supportive network of friends, of people who had also suffered from mental illness, who couldn't reach out and help him.

Jeff Healey lost his sight when he was just one year of age. Born with cancer in both eyes, he has gone on to become a respected broadcaster, musician and one of the country's leading experts on vintage jazz.

I think what is important is how well one is able to apply oneself to—in my case—the actual art of performing on stage whether you are blind or not, whether you can walk or talk or not … any perceived or sometimes not so perceived handicaps we all have should be thrown aside. What matters is how good you are at what you do, and how you relate to an audience. If your success is solely based on your handicap, it's very short-lived.

Dr. Euclid J. Herie, former president of the Canadian National Institute for the Blind and the World Blind Union, lost his sight at age sixteen—but certainly has never lost his vision.

It took me a very long time to come to terms with the fact that my blindness was my persona. It was me. It was what I was. And I was going to be blind all the days of my life. So

I had better get to like it. I had better get to like myself. And believe in myself.

Many of the great minds and insightful thinkers have had some kind of handicap or flaw that in the end steered them toward success, even greatness. At the time of my conversation with Professor Edward O. Wilson, he had just published his riveting work *Consilience*. The word is an arcane one that means the "jumping together" of different fields of knowledge. Aside from being a genius, Wilson is also known as the Ant Man. "Every child has a 'bug phase.' I just didn't grow out of mine," Wilson explained. He went to fifteen different schools from kindergarten to Grade 12 because his father moved around a lot. The many uprootings had an effect on Wilson:

> It made it difficult for me to get in with groups of kids and make lifelong friends. I tended to turn to nature, which was always available, and I became more of an amateur naturalist.

Wilson lost the vision in his right eye in a fishing accident when he was seven, but the handicap proved fortuitous:

> I didn't have the depth of vision you would need to be a bird watcher, but I did have very sharp vision in my other eye, and the result was I soon decided to devote myself to the little things that you could hold between thumb and fore- finger and study up close. It was a very appropriate choice for me to make.

I decided somewhere that I wouldn't be left behind. And I never have been and I don't intend to be.
DR. EUCLID J. HERIE,
FORMER PRESIDENT OF CNIB

133

He's always made the best of his circumstances. "I was in my sixties before I realized I could probably have qualified as a person with a handicap."

It was against all odds that Sir Edmund Hillary would be the first—along with his Sherpa companion—to climb Mount Everest in 1953. One of the twentieth century's greatest heroes started life as a skinny kid with back problems. "Problems are a part of the routine of life; one just has to overcome them."

Entrepreneur Sir Richard Branson turned his dyslexia to lucrative advantage. He always had a hard time reading a balance sheet and coping with financial statements. In fact, he confessed that, because of his limitations, he did not really even know the difference between net and gross income. To compensate, he learned to trust his instincts about people and the marketplace, which he says has greatly helped move his Virgin group of companies into the monetary stratosphere:

> I have to be more methodical than people who are not dyslexic. I have to keep notes and write lists. I think part of my success is that I take notes, and follow through and get everything done.

Elvis Stojko is far from disabled, but at several crucial moments in his skating career he's been dealt some difficult cards. No matter what the circumstances, he can't afford a "why me" mentality. Self-pity—even for a fraction of a second—can be costly to Elvis:

> I can't sit there and think, "Why me, why me?" I have to deal with what I have. The biggest thing I've learned over the years

is to deal with what you have and not with what you think you should have.

What Willie O'Ree had was a talent for hockey. The man who was called the "Jackie Robinson of hockey" broke the colour barrier in the National Hockey League. He remembers that day:

> When I stepped on the ice January 18, 1958, and became the first black hockey player to play in the NHL, my main concern was to go out, play a good game against the Montreal Canadiens at the Forum, which is exactly what we did. Being the first black NHL player never even occurred to me.

There were, however, racist comments whenever he played in the United States. Willie was also dealing with a serious physical handicap. While playing junior hockey he had been struck by a puck in the right eye. He lost ninety-seven percent of his vision in that eye, and still went on to play in the big leagues. "I loved the game so much, I just said, 'I can still see out of my other eye, so I guess I'll just go out there and play.'" Although his career wasn't long—he played just forty-three games with the Boston Bruins—there wouldn't be another black player in the NHL for twenty-five years.

Joni Mitchell discovered she had polio at the age of nine; this was, unfortunately, just before the Salk vaccine was discovered. Soon she was paralyzed and was placed in what she described as a "terrifying" hospital for victims of the crippling disease. She still shudders as she recalls the sound of the pumping of the iron lungs. Joni was told she might never walk again. Although she did survive it all, she gave up running and playing sports and took up dance. "I celebrated my legs," she said, "but I turned to grace instead of speed." The experience was powerful:

> Every time you rise up from some near-death encounter, you come back stronger and hopefully more full of life. It either makes you or breaks you.

All these people have had to play the cards they were dealt, but sometimes things happen to other people and you're left holding their cards too. Some of my guests have endured excruciating grief, have survived by overcoming immense adversity. So often grief stops us in our tracks and immobilizes us. Thomas Moore, a psychotherapist who has written many books on caring for the soul, had a conversation with me about loss and grief:

> We have to use grief as an opportunity to become more humane. We do need to feel more—not less. We need these experiences—they are our humanity. Loss is part of our life story.

But the old adage that time heals all wounds may not be comfort enough. David Stiller, who lost his daughter Jill to suicide, puts it this way: "Time doesn't heal. Living heals." Our memories are different than our experiences. And in many ways, Stiller believes, that may be an important survival mechanism:

One of the things about when people say "time heals" concerned me because I thought maybe that meant that I'd forget—and I don't want to forget Jill. If healing was that, then I never wanted healing because I never wanted to forget. But by living, and talking about it, and moving through life and involving ourselves in the pain of others when they have it, it keeps us in touch.

A beautiful woman by the name of Lata Pada, a teacher and dancer, had gone home to India to prepare for a dance performance. Her husband and daughters were to follow a few days later. They boarded the ill-fated Air India flight 182 that was downed by a terrorist's bomb. They all perished. It's a loss of a proportion that few of us can fathom. As Lata talked of her loss, there was a calmness and serenity that confounded me. From where did that quiet grace emerge? She anwered:

> They are very much in my soul. It's this box of treasure that I dip into every day. I savour them. I retrieve them one by one when the days are dark and dismal. In each of the young women that I teach, I see aspects of my daughters. I celebrate in their happiness and I celebrate in their success. They bring a lot of joy into my life.

As Thomas Moore explained, it's very hard to deal with death when everything around you denies it:

Life is a very delicate thing, so there is no point being negative about it.

SHANIA TWAIN, SINGER

It's very difficult. And we have no support. As a society, we deal with death every single day—and I don't just mean the actual death of people, family or friends, I mean our own daily small deaths, our failures, our mistakes, broken relationships, divorces.

Denny Doherty, an original member of the legendary musical group The Mamas & The Papas, lost his wife to cancer and described how he coped:

It hurts, but somebody said an interesting thing … to me: "When you get to these places, don't veer off. Put your head against it, lean into it and get through it."

Slowing Down to the Speed of Life

I've always believed that the secret to living and thriving in a noisy,
busy world is to have a quiet inside—now you don't get
that without some effort.
MAURICE STRONG, U.N. ADVISER

When Maurice Strong, who spends more time on planes than off them in his work for the United Nations, needs some downtime he comes home to Canada and to the quiet of a country home. Quiet is a rare commodity these days, but at my cabin on a lake near Wadena, I often find I can't sleep for the first few days because of the sound of the silence. There are no sirens, nor is there the constant, almost reassuring din of traffic that seems to have become the soundtrack of my life in the urban jungle. You see, if I hear the sounds, I know I'm part of something larger. Even as a kid I was always filling up the void with music or endless phone conversations—it seemed to soothe that awkward phase of adolescence when you're too old for dolls and too young to date. Today, an unwatched TV often fills my house with familiar voices even though I'm neither watching nor listening. For me, the sounds of silence were always frightening. In my business, silence—or as we call it, "dead air"—means there's a problem: the guest is paralyzed with fear, or perhaps I've lost my train of thought and as I scramble to find it, the guest sits patiently and quietly waiting. No chatter in my earpiece might also signal a lost connection to the control room or that the person I'm interviewing has disappeared into some technical ether.

Increasingly, though, I long for the solace of the silence. Maybe I've just filled my predetermined quota of noise with all those years covering Question Period in the House of Commons and sitting in studios with an earpiece connecting me to the clatter, chaos and commotion of the so-called control room. This does not mean that I intend to take a vow of silence, move into the nearest convent or somehow live apart from friends or the real world. But finding a quieter outside from time to time may be a prerequisite to finding that quiet inside. In fact, I think you need the quiet time so that you can begin to realize you need it. How many times do you silently scream, "Give me some peace and quiet," as you politely say out loud, "Please, just give me a moment, I need to think this through," and put your head in your hands as if to protect it from the onslaught of further distraction?

Philosopher Umberto Eco always takes time to think before he talks—even on television. So when our conversation turned to technology and human interaction, he spoke instead of our need for quiet:

> We have become more able to think in noise. But I discover more and more that because I live in a noisy world of universal information, I appreciate more and more the moments of soli-

I do have to have that private dialogue, that private time with what it is that I am wrestling.
KEN DANBY, ARTIST

tude. That's why I travel. Eight hours of flight is eight hours of solitude. I'd use the train instead of the car if there were not the cell telephone people sitting across from me. With the mail, I am not disturbing people. With the cell phone, I am disturbing people everywhere around me. To use the cell phone, obliging me to listen to all your personal problems while I am reading, is an act of violence against my privacy. It is not a status symbol. A cell phone is, in fact, a sign of social inferiority. If you were Mr. Rockefeller, you would not have a cell telephone.

And the problem, Eco says, with our work-obsessed society is that "all work, all the time" has become a kind of status symbol, and technology has made it all the more possible:

The soul has an unforgiving need for moments of magic.
THOMAS MOORE, AUTHOR

We live life at such a speed that was unknown to our ancestors, and if my grandmother had to live at my speed, she would have died at the age of twenty.

Technology is a wonderful advancement, but it makes it increasingly difficult to find peace and quiet, either inside or out. Even scientists such as the world's leading astrophysicist, Hubert Reeves, know when to eschew gadgets:

I hate the watch. I find the watch like a dictator telling me what to do. You have to have one, but when you go to the country, I live without any sense of time and no schedule.

More time means, increasingly, more time to work. I can't live without a watch because in television every second counts. I often wonder, however, which came first, my need for structure and order or the work itself?

～～

I think as a culture we've got very anxious about silence—we need to fill it with a lot of noise. Hopefully we can choose a profession that will help us find that stillness—there is a stillness in me, but sometimes I lose the key to that room. BEN KINGSLEY, ACTOR

One of the most important things is to find a little bit of space and peace somewhere and try to listen to within. Turn off the radio, turn off the telly and just be quiet and listen to yourself, and then try and act on it, whatever it is. SARAH FERGUSON, DUCHESS OF YORK

It seems to me that in the last decade we were really focused on "entertainment." The whole world seems to be trying to find something to do—let's go out and be entertained. Racing, racing to find the next thing. This thought just sort of came to me one night: Why are we always trying to find something to do? Why don't we just stay home and be together? CHARLIE MAJOR, SINGER AND MUSICIAN

～～

Once in a while, there's a conversation that makes me just a little uncomfortable—some might even say defensive. Dr. Barbara Killinger is a psychologist and the author of *Workaholics: The Respectable Addicts.* When a producer in the office proposed the interview, I think it was a not-so-subtle message to me. I would read the book, see the error of my ways and stop demanding that they all work twenty-four hours a day, seven days a week, as I was doing. Not surprisingly, workaholics tend to hire other workaholics. Predictably, as I read the book, I reacted somewhat skeptically to the rather sweeping characterizations. Still, this was not a pretty picture.

And perhaps the most frightening point—and it had not been so obvious to me—was that workaholics are perfectionists. Now this is something I've always taken pride in. I agree with what Martha Stewart told me was her operating mantra: "To err is human. To correct is absolutely imperative."

Yes, Ms. Martha is a woman after my own heart. We nodded knowingly, both on camera and off, as we regaled each other with stories of endless days and the perils facing women in business. We agreed that we must reject mediocrity, strive to be perfectionists, be demanding, have high standards and expect no less of those around us. I actually believe this, and even after reading Dr. Killinger's book, I still share the sentiment. I suspect I've just worked in one too many places where the mindset is about keeping the standards and the expectations down and where the "it's not in my job description" mentality prevails. That said, I believe Killinger's insights are valuable in assessing whether we are just busy people coping with the pressures

I no longer expect the kind of perfectionism from myself that would drive me before. I am perfectly willing to put up with the fact that I make mistakes and I'm imperfect.

Michael Korda, editor

of an ever more demanding work world or whether we create the circumstances that feed our obsession. Dr. Killinger explained:

> Perfectionism always leads to obsession, and the obsession is to work. Workaholics cannot not work, which is ironic because they want to control everything, but it is controlling them. They are very concerned that they will be seen to be lazy, and they feel that if they get off the gerbil wheel, somebody will think that of them.

Okay. So far, not so good. The "they" was sounding a lot like me. Workaholic? I was building a business, doing live interviews five nights a week, giving speeches, travelling and hosting charity events. You know the old saying, "If you want something done, ask a busy person." But despite my claims that I was just one of those very busy people, the words on the page forced me to take a second look. If Dr. Killinger was right, I was in trouble, because I was seeking perfection in a business where perfection is impossible and where, worse yet, all our human flaws are apparent to everyone. Dr. Killinger made this observation:

> Workaholics get hooked on adrenaline and go in to work on Saturday and Sunday because it is the one place they really feel important and alive. They have an external frame of reference and see themselves through other people's eyes. The doing/performing part is huge. They lose the being/feeling side. If your feelings don't work, half of your personality is "knocked

out." When your feeling stops working, so does your intuition, and then you lose the big picture.

All right, no changing the channel, folks, just because you don't like the reflection on the screen. Of course, we all have crises and deadlines and busy periods. But after this discussion I began to think about the long hours we were putting in at my production company and tried to separate the real demands of the work from the self-imposed ones. A work ethic is a good thing, but it never hurts to do a reality check—the warnings are there for all of us to see. As Dr. Killinger noted, workaholics get so paranoid, they even stop taking holidays.

Author and respected anthropologist of everyday life Margaret Visser says holidays shouldn't be about getting away from life, they should be part of life:

> It's bizarre behaviour ... that our lives are something we have to escape. I have to work all year to be able to go somewhere beautiful for two weeks. Think of the word "vacate."

Dr. Stanley Coren, the expert on sleep, says never mind vacation, we seldom afford ourselves a good night's rest:

> The culprit is society's attitude toward sleep. We have
> this whole notion that somehow the movers and the shakers
> in society are people who go without sleep. Certainly it's
> a Hollywood stereotype—John Wayne; or we're always

We're not supposed to be one thing. On the contrary. We're just supposed to be in balance.

GLORIA STEINEM,
FEMINIST AND AUTHOR

being told that Thomas Edison or da Vinci only slept four hours a night.

Thomas Moore says the pressures of the technological speedup have far-reaching consequences.

When you make a statement like "We have to work, we have to be productive, we have to get things done," well, there's some anxiety in that, isn't there? "We have to"—that's an anxious statement. I think we have an anxiety in our culture about productivity and about work, as though we justify our existence, as though we find the meaning in our lives, through being productive. That doesn't have to be. As a matter of fact, I would think that slavery to being productive is what makes it difficult to be married today, it makes it difficult to hold families together. I think that there is a relationship between that deep, deep work ethic and that loss of soul.

So, can a highly productive life lead to success if all else in your life fails? That question was at the heart of a fascinating conversation I had with Canada's foremost Jungian analyst and psychologist, Marion Woodman, a woman often called "the midwife of souls." It was a busy day; we were prerecording several shows and I was, as usual, on fast-forward. As we sat down on set to begin, it seemed that once again a messenger had been dispatched to try to get my attention. Marion Woodman went right for the workaholic's Achilles' heel:

You can say, "I can't get off the treadmill," but eventually a symptom will pull you off. Then the soul comes in and says, "Okay, here is a symptom, deal with this symptom," and if you don't, eventually you will have to deal with it at some different level and the illness will give you time to change your behaviour. Or not. If you choose not to, then you have to put up with the next symptom.

Then another messenger arrived. Neil Peart, the drummer for the band Rush, is also an adventure traveller and upon his return from cycling through West Africa, he wrote a book called *The Masked Rider*. During our conversation about his trip he explained: "A bicycle is an instrument that moves along at people speed." It was that phrase, "people speed," that once again triggered thoughts about slowing down to the speed of life.

Despite all the messages and warnings, I, obviously, still wasn't listening—until I was taught a painful lesson. It took only a few seconds. While hurrying out the door en route to the next appointment, I fell down the stairs in my own home, snapping my leg and cracking my ankle. I was confined to bed for the better part of six weeks and then was encumbered with a cast, wheelchair and walker for another six. My mother, in a vain attempt to be supportive, suggested that this was an act of God designed to give me some much-needed rest and a chance to limp off the treadmill, at least briefly. And, she promised, there was a greater purpose to all of this: the accident was intended to teach me about patience, something that has

Television is a passive medium. All you have to do is click it off. Turn it off. And there's really a profound silence.
RICHARD FORD, AUTHOR

149

always been in short supply in my world. In reality, the frustration of being so wholly dependent was provoking little more than anger and tears. Eventually, I came to admit that I was not superwoman, that I could not carry on as if nothing had happened and that the internal turmoil was using up the energy needed just to accomplish life's basic tasks. With all those weeks of staring at the wall—or worse yet, a TV screen filled with reruns—I eventually learned that patience is a tool to help manage the unexpected. It was a great feeling to discover that I could still learn something other than a fact or piece of information!

While it was only a broken leg, the experience gave me enough time to think about priorities. In the wee small hours of the morning, I would lie awake because of the pain, and my thoughts would turn to how short life really is. How many times had I heard that cliché, without ever stopping to think about it? I recalled a couple of conversations on this very topic. Eric Idle, of Monty Python fame, told of surviving two earthquakes. "I kind of enjoy them. It reminds you that you're on a planet. That's what we should be doing—reminding ourselves that we are here and we may be gone tomorrow. Life is precious. Live it now. And don't mess around and postpone things."

The late Brian Moore, author, was in a boating accident when he was just twenty-six years old. "Life is finite, and if you want to be happy, try and do the things that you really want to do," he advised. "It's worth it."

Imagine your final moments; imagine you have just six months to live. What would be most important? With whom would you spend

Drink life. Live each moment with passion.

Wei Chen, broadcaster

150

your precious time, and where? And what would you be doing? Without a doubt, your priorities would change. I'm sure you would care less whether people liked you or approved of you, and you'd probably be less obsessed with power or money, although the latter would be far more useful in realizing your dreams.

In my travels, some of which have taken me into harm's way, I've sometimes had those conversations with myself. Only three or four times have I truly feared for my life, once during a riot in Argentina during the Falklands War and again when we were being held by the so-called security forces, who already had journalists' blood on their hands. And once in El Salvador, where the flags of neutrality flying from our van's windows meant precious little to either side in a bloody and protracted civil war. But even during turbulence on a plane, I always try to strike a deal with that powerful being "up there," that if He or She will just get me through this one, I promise to change my ways and be a better person, write the letters I've been meaning to write, turn the other cheek, stop to smell the roses, etc.

None of us is ever sure whether today will be our last day, and if it were, whether we would be satisfied with our priorities and choices. I can only hope that I will find the strength of character that I have seen emerge in friends when they have faced their own death or wrestled with a frightening disability. I've witnessed their metamorphosis as they learn to live in the moment and begin to focus on what and who matters most. Living for today might suggest a devil-may-care, damn-the-consequences approach, but selfishness is not the point—making

It's unbelievable how quickly we can be gone so don't sweat the small stuff—because it's all small stuff.

TERRI CLARK, SINGER

each moment matter is. Conversations with those who have experienced this are like my mother's voice gently chiding me to listen up. Life is short.

Diana Krall spends a lot of time flying to performances around the world. And though she's not a confident flyer, she maintains an irreverent sense of humour. She explains how a religious girl copes:

> You never know how long it will last. I'm clutching my cross in one hand and a vodka tonic in the other on the plane. I'm religious, okay, but I like a cocktail! ... You have to live your life somewhat in the moment because you don't know, so you try to live without pettiness and crap—it's unnecessary.

John Allen Cameron is one of Canada's most popular performers. He too has been inspired by a tragedy that befell close friends to learn to live for today:

> I agree with the old saying, "Yesterday is a cancelled cheque and tomorrow is a postdated cheque." Today is the only thing that's spendable. Do what you have to do in life.

Perhaps for the actor, living in the moment is just the nature of the

We're here for such a short time ... we've got to make the best of it.

MAEVE BINCHY, AUTHOR

work. But it has also become Gordon Pinsent's motto for living life:

> It's the moment we are living. It's the moment we're having, not the one we hope to have, not the one we're going to have, or maybe will have if we go through the right door. It is truly the moment we're living.

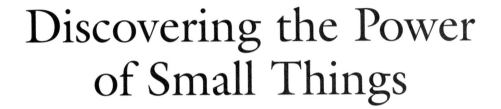

Chapter Nine

Discovering the Power of Small Things

It is that moment that
you will remember.

PHIL COLLINS, SINGER

It's the experience of joy and satisfaction—a moment of connection or understanding—fleeting but powerfully etched on your mind. When drummer turned solo singer Phil Collins joined me in the studio for a conversation, it was at a point in his life when he was beginning to take a little time off and enjoy time with his family. He told a wonderful story about trying to teach his children the importance of recognizing and capturing those special moments:

> I had a conversation with my daughter about "how your shutter goes off"—how and why you will remember a particular event from your childhood that your mother and father don't remember. Your "camera" goes off, theirs doesn't. One day Lily said, "Dad, I think my camera just went off!"

In dozens of interviews I have experienced that feeling of being able to reach in and touch, even for a moment, the core of that person sitting across from me. It may be empathy for a personal circumstance or simply grasping and translating the idea or passion that moves that person. As the late Margaret Laurence once said, you must be able to feel in your heart's core the reality of others. As a writer and creator of characters, this ability was central to her work. And it is key in my job too because, as a professional observer and solicitor of stories, I must give real-life characters a stage on which they can, with comfort and confidence, tell their story. But it seems to me this approach would be helpful regardless of your walk of life.

When singer and songwriter Mary-Chapin Carpenter released her song "A Place in the World," I asked her to explain the title. She replied that you find your place only because of the power of small moments:

> The moments I am referring to are those where something
> happens to make you feel like you know why you're doing
> what you're doing, who you are, and where you are—they are
> moments of happiness, but mostly of clarity … It's as simple as
> a lover saying something to you in a certain way, it's the way
> light falls across a room … It's a catalyst for those moments
> and all of a sudden you feel a peace, or a contentment. What
> I mean by a place in the world is not something that you all
> of a sudden find, and from then on you're there, but rather
> it is something that is always evolving with you.

I sing to calm myself down.

ART GARFUNKEL, SINGER

AND SONGWRITER

BB King, a hopeless romantic, was brief but eloquent on the power of small things in his life: "When a lady really cares about you, just certain little things she can say—a little touch, a little smooch on your chin—means more than I can tell you."

⌒⌒

I would like to consider myself a spiritual person and look to every opportunity to be spiritually engaged, but that can come in a very casual circumstance, you know. Sometimes it's just a lovely dinner with friends, sometimes it's a very simple every-day kind of thing. LOREENA MCKENNITT, SINGER AND SONGWRITER

Simple things. Just the niceties that we used to have. Smiling. It's not even a matter of saying anything, just smiling at someone. MICHELE LEE, ACTRESS

We don't need to be persuaded that violence or immorality is powerful. But I think that we have to be persuaded again and again of the power of the small act—a kindness, the small act of love. ANNE MICHAELS, AUTHOR

A lot of my books begin from the smallest thing—a phrase or even a bit of music or, in the case of *Ragtime*, a moment of desperation. I'd been working for a year and nothing happened. And then I was staring at the wall, so I started writing about the wall … and then I hopped along from one image to the next. E.L. DOCTOROW, AUTHOR

⌒⌒

I am grateful to have grown up in a house where reading books was encouraged and I shared Pulitzer Prize–winning author Anna Quindlen's joy of the written word: "I had this sense of interior wanderlust, even as a child, and that's the amazing thing about books," she said. Anna understood that books can offer those moments of insight and joy:

> I've always tried to write about the power of small things. To show you how we fashion our lives in those small moments and how we should treasure and honour them.

As a family we played cards and talked (this was pre-TV, and yes, Virginia, there was such a time). There was no art gallery in Wadena, nor did the opera or ballet come anywhere near our town, never mind our province. But through conversations and books I was transported to magical places, and along the way I met some amazing people—characters in the books and in the stories I was told. Mrs. Fair, a sometime babysitter, had pictures and souvenirs from distant corners of the world. So did my uncle, who had been in India during the war. My parents and grandparents had stories of other things and places. And there was always the encyclopedia—with pictures. And to me, that was art.

Our home was full of books so I had to become a reader. I had no choice.

JACK MCCLELLAND,

PUBLISHER

In a conversation with W.O. Mitchell, I had one of those "camera goes off" moments when he gave art its proper context:

Art—either the appreciation of it or the practice of it—is the only thing that humans do for its own sake.

Too few things in life do we do just for the sake of it: smelling the coffee, knitting a scarf, reading a work of fiction, dallying over a picture—even a crayon drawing taped to the fridge door—or listening to music without cleaning or driving at the same time. Some have even suggested art is a basic human need. Sherwin B. Nuland, a surgeon and medical historian, argues that there is a biological imperative to nurture the human spirit with art:

Small is good and small is a decent way to think. It's about making choices.
Jann Arden, singer and songwriter

Things that have to do with beauty have no survival value. We see beauty, we create beauty, we value beauty. That is a spiritual need that only the human mind can conceive of.

It wasn't until the end of my first year in university that I actually ventured abroad—a summer in France because, at that moment, I had my heart set on becoming a French teacher. I sensed history in the weathered stone walls of buildings, heard languages spoken—both mine and theirs—in a way I had never heard before, and I saw art at the Louvre, just for the sake of it. This was very different from the Alan Nagy paint-by-number sets that had allowed even those of us who can't colour inside the lines to express ourselves and take pride in the creative act. But I've always believed that the experience of art or culture need not occur in concert halls or famous foreign capitals. It can be found very close to home. And you can start small. Violinist Pinchas Zukerman agrees: "What I recommend to parents is just give your child an instrument—any instrument. Just give it to them. Even if they are holding it while watching Saturday cartoons. Just see what happen."

My parents did try to instill a little culture with the dreaded piano lessons. I took them—reluctantly—for years but finally won the battle to be granted my freedom from all the after-school practising (but not until my parents judged I had learned the importance of a little discipline and stick-to-it-iveness). Those skills—and even the piano lessons—have come in very handy over the years, and so, as usual, I concede that my parents were right, as they were about so many things.

Diana Krall put her piano lessons to professional use and agrees that exposure to music is a good thing for any child:

> The music has enabled me to do things. The most important thing I had was music at home. Don't shove it down their throats, just *play* it. And take your kids to see live music—that is really important.

When actor Tony Curtis first came to the United States, he didn't know the language, so he would draw or paint to express himself:

> Painting was a way to express my feelings. It's another way of screaming into space, another way of exchanging feelings.

If you don't have the arts in a society, it will become a jungle. We won't be people. We'll be animals.

PINCHAS ZUKERMAN,
VIOLIN VIRTUOSO

~

My mother took me to everything—ballets, concerts, operas, symphonies—even when I was five. I saw the most extraordinary people. I even saw Rachmaninoff when I was fourteen. I remember he was a very tall man, very imposing. He sat down and glared at the audience for a long time, until they all stopped coughing and became absolutely silent. And then those great hands hit the piano. That's about all I remember—but I learned how to shut an audience up! CHRISTOPHER PLUMMER, ACTOR

I learn something every time I see the plays. The plays are so rich—so as you grow, they grow. So you see different things in it. So, for instance, if you are having trouble with your parents, because they are elderly, and you go to a performance of *King Lear*, you see it from a different point of view than if you are young—say a teenager—and looking at *King Lear*. It's the words, of course, that make this insight—the way he expresses the inexpressible. RICHARD MONETTE, ARTISTIC DIRECTOR OF THE STRATFORD FESTIVAL

We go to the theatre to learn about ourselves. NEIL SIMON, PLAYWRIGHT

~

We are all surprised by the accidental lessons that exposure to the arts may teach us or our children. Playwrights, artists and performers insist that art also teaches about human nature and civility. Teacher and violin virtuoso Isaac Stern made an eloquent case:

> That is what great art is all about—constant examination and a hopefulness for the betterment of the human condition between us.

Artist Ken Danby says living without some understanding of, experience of or exposure to art will leave us, as adults, incomplete:

> Without art, we're handicapped. We're living a stifled, barren existence. Art is a necessity. Art is an absolutely essential part of our enlightenment process. We cannot—as a species, as a society, as a civilization—regard ourselves as being enlightened without the arts.

Consuming and viewing art has its own reward, and sometimes we can find entertainment in the strangest of places. Frank McCourt found it in New York:

> I'm a spectator in New York. I love standing on street corners and praying for fender-benders, and they yell four-letter words about each other's mother and they're just about to get out and hit each other, but then the light turns green and off they go—and I've had fifteen seconds of pure drama.

McCourt may find "art" on a street corner, but when it comes right down to it, he seeks out the traditional as well:

> Shakespeare is like mashed potatoes—you can never have enough. Like jewels in my mouth, his poetry. Yes, Shakespeare is the man.

And we needn't be so judgemental about what qualifies as art. The world's most prolific songstress, Nana Mouskouri, explained to me her rather eclectic tastes. She had just been to a Guns N' Roses concert, but she's also a Bob Dylan fan, as she is of the music of Bryan Adams:

> Each one has its own magic. Its own feeling. It's the world itself you penetrate, and you live with it and you take what you need from them.

Communicate. Present the work. Nurture the response so that people feel comfortable. Don't cater to the audience ... inspire the audience.
KEN DANBY, ARTIST

❧

Many of those special moments in our lives are humorous ones. Sharing an inside joke is an intimate act, said Sir George Martin:

> I think humour is certainly an important part of our lives. Music certainly is the most important, but, gosh, you've got to laugh or life isn't worth anything.

To explore comedy is to destroy it. It's fragile.
FRANK SHUSTER, COMEDIAN

Sir George, the man who discovered the Beatles and went on to become one of the most influential and respected producers in the history of popular music, made his final contribution to the world of music by inviting the most unlikely cast of stars to perform and record Beatles tunes. Comedian Jim Carrey does "I Am the Walrus," Robin Williams has a bizarre take on "Come Together" and Goldie Hawn does a torchy rendition of "A Hard Day's Night," with her trademark giggle sprinkled throughout. Sir George just couldn't resist the sound. "I'd go anywhere for a giggle from Goldie Hawn."

It was, for him, just one of those moments, and we need to listen for them in our lives. "The listening process is what life is about," said Pinchas Zukerman. The violin virtuoso explained the importance of both listening and hearing. Listening is what the audience does, hearing is what the performer does. If music is about both listening and hearing, so too is much of our social or personal interaction—at least it should be. Urban satirist Fran Liebowitz once said that the opposite of talking isn't listening, it's waiting. How true. So often people are just waiting to take their turn or for someone to relinquish the floor. It's like those annoying moments at cocktail parties when you are engaged in a very serious debate about the future of the world, music, art or politics and you notice the other participant in this terribly meaningful conversation is looking just past you, nodding meaningfully but with eyes darting quickly in search of someone more important. The person is not listening except in that he or she is waiting for the next pause at which to make an exit. And as I mentioned earlier, listening is, I have discovered, the key ingredient in the art of conversation. Listening is also a crucial part of being successful in life, love and work.

Humour is by far the most significant activity of the brain.

Dr. Edward de Bono, author

Sarah Ferguson said during our conversation that had she taken the time to read her own feelings, many of the troubles she encountered—the scandals and her reaction to them—could have been avoided. "I wasn't listening. I wasn't listening to what my inner self was telling me."

Actor Jack Klugman told a profoundly sad story about what happens when we don't hear what is really being said:

> I used to think my father died from lack of money. I went to see my father in the hospital when I was twelve years old. He was in a ward with thirty other people and he kept saying to my mother, "Take me home. They aren't listening to me." He died two days later. Recently I spoke to doctors who were graduating from Mount Sinai, and I realized what my father had said, and I said, "I always thought my father died of poverty, but he didn't. Look what he said: 'They don't listen to me.' It doesn't cost anything to listen. So if I come into your office, don't be so quick to tell me to take off my shirt. Don't reach for the stethoscope. Talk to me. I might even tell you what's wrong with me."

I had to learn how to listen more, and we had to keep fighting for our relationship, because relationships need to be worked on.

RICK HANSEN, ACTIVIST

Dr. Robert Buckman says he's seen the same thing happen too many times:

> One of the things that you really need to know how to do is to listen. You've got to be a good listener. People get this thing

that they ought to know what to say ... isn't there some rule, some magic formula—sadly, there isn't. Understand their agenda so they can talk about what they want to talk about. And you're allowed to say, "I don't know what to say."

The idea of talking less and listening more provoked a story from actor and director Saul Rubinek about working with director Clint Eastwood on *The Unforgiven*:

What was extraordinary about him was that instead of having the kind of ego that most of the directors I've worked with over twenty-five years who micro-managed every aspect of the production have had, his attitude was, rather than have his vision met and realized, to have his vision transcended, and in order to do such a thing, he shut up a lot.

Living Out Loud

Children speak the truth—until a certain age
when they learn how to lie.
FRANK MCCOURT, AUTHOR

We live in a culture of deception. Presidential denials, advertising, TV plot lines, not to mention the lies lovers tell. And then there are journalists, cops and doctors who must all lie from time to time, even though, we hope, for good reason. Telling the truth is almost always risky. My parents used to say that confession would not help us avoid punishment, but it might soften the sentence. We usually spilled, hoping for mercy. But later in life, you eventually realize that saying what you mean can have unintended consequences. It can even be career-limiting. Of this I have plenty of personal experience. Speaking truth to power—or even to those in charge—is the premise upon which the theory of journalism is built, although these days it is seldom practised. Still, many of the people I've spoken with over the years have eventually concluded that it's the only way to go—in spite of the consequences.

Martin Sheen, an outspoken activist on social justice, has been arrested and jailed many times for his public protests:

> I love my country personally enough to risk its wrath by point-
> ing out the dark spots. And you have to take your lumps when
> you point out the naked emperor. You're going to be the first
> one to put words on the truth, it's going to cost you some-
> thing. It has to cost you something. Anything worthwhile
> is expensive.

Those, like Sheen, with status and celebrity can more easily afford the costs of those risks. On the other hand, Booker Prize–winning author Margaret Atwood says high-profile people have more opportunity— and more pressure—to do just that:

> If you, the citizen, don't raise your hand, the consequences can
> just keep rolling. To me, that is what any citizen should do.
> But I am a freelancer and I believe freelancers of any kind—not
> just writers like myself—don't have a boss. Therefore they are
> free to speak out on issues and say things that lots of other
> people think but if they said them, they'd be fired. And that is
> the long and the short of it. You are often called upon more
> than other people.

Legitimate and necessary criticism is often muted in the cacoph-ony of shouting and yelling that is part of our media-saturated society. And trying to be heard above the din is difficult. That said, I feel that

I think businesspeople have an obligation to let the world know where their heads are at. I have some strongly held views and I believe in articulating them.

Izzy Asper, businessman

it is the duty of all to try to speak your mind, and, when possible, to be honest, while sparing the feelings of others when no harm will be done. Fortunately, a key part of my mother's lesson to me was to speak your mind, but only once that mind is informed. Columnist Dalton Camp says it is especially true in politics:

> Too many of us want to play a role without wanting to do our homework. We want to speak out about issues without really forming some intelligent opinion. We have freedom of speech, but we have a responsibility to learn, and it's not simple, and one side is not all right and one side is not all wrong.

But as a society, it seems we often don't want politicians to tell the truth, especially if they've changed their minds. The journalist is the first to accuse the politician of doing an about-face, when, in fact, it may be an informed change of heart. Former New Brunswick premier Frank McKenna, who won a clean sweep of the Legislative Assembly in 1987, took his share of heat for his straightforward approach:

> There were many times I put my foot in my mouth. Sometimes you can have all the facts but you come to the wrong conclusion ... Every time we get into a major public policy issue, usually the information is good enough that you're right, but sometimes you're just wrong. And if you then stand up and say, "I was wrong," you get ridiculed, and after you get ridiculed a few times, you start to wonder if you

Why don't we just talk about stuff that matters to us instead of stuff that doesn't matter to us?
PETER GZOWSKI,
BROADCASTER AND
JOURNALIST

I know what I want and I state what I want. Just say what you mean and hopefully everything will work out.
MICHELE LEE, ACTRESS

should ever admit you're wrong, and just plug on instead. If you're wrong, you should be able to stand up, admit it, take your medicine and fix it.

A great conversation comes to mind that speaks to the necessity of telling the truth and the consequences of not telling the truth. Ben Bradlee, the affable former executive editor of the *Washington Post*, backed his reporters Bob Woodward and Carl Bernstein, ably assisted by the still anonymous Deep Throat, throughout their historic pursuit of the truth. And even today, nothing is more likely to spark a debate about truth than the defining period in U.S. politics that we now refer to simply as Watergate.

Bradlee and I had a passionate discussion about truth in journalism, but also about the need for all of us to tell the truth. Just a few minutes into our conversation, Bradlee was already animated, stabbing the table with his finger:

> You've got to stop people from lying, you really do. If journalism has any real justification, it's that you are looking for the truth, so the people that obstruct the truth—that lie about it— are really the people who ought to be punished.

And paraphrasing the words of Shakespeare, Bradlee declared:

> The truth will out, and I'm as sure of it as I'm sitting here—it could take eighteen or twenty years, but it will out.

I just tell the truth but not just the facts. I take the bare bones and add a bit of muscle, fat and gloss.

FARLEY MOWAT, AUTHOR

Sometimes truth-telling takes real courage—and willingness to risk. Dr. Barry Armstrong and his wife, Jennifer, were the so-called whistle-blowers in the Somalia scandal. Jennifer released to the media a letter her husband had written her that described the execution of an unarmed Somali man by Canadian soldiers. Barry had tried to go through the proper chain of command and put his concerns and grievances on record. But no one wanted to hear the gruesome facts, which Barry recalled when we talked:

> That night changed my whole feeling about the military forever. It was the shock, looking at the body and the wounds, realizing he had been shot in the back, he had lived for some minutes, he was probably lying helpless on the ground, and then they finished him off when they shot him in the head to kill him. Many people in high places, given high responsibilities, were quite happy to accept murder. I was not, and I realized I would never ever sleep again if I stayed part of this conspiracy.

Sometimes truth-tellers are underestimated because we've come to believe that people put self-interest ahead of principle. According to Barry, the military underestimated him:

> They didn't understand that I was willing to give up all my money, I was willing to give up my house, I was willing to give up my family, my career, my name as a doctor, I was willing to give up everything so that the military could be improved.

So it wasn't really a fight, because we weren't playing by the same rules.

I asked Barry how he and Jennifer explained all of this to their young children. Barry replied:

Their grandmother, a kindergarten teacher, read them the story *The Emperor's New Clothes,* about a high-ranking person who puts on airs and thinks that he is wearing beautiful clothes and isn't, but there is a small boy who knows the truth and speaks it. And I told them, "In this situation, it's not clothing, it's a capital crime, and I'm the small boy. I see what everyone else says, but I know the truth." At least our kids know that you can fight City Hall or higher.

⌇⌇

Nothing is black and white, but if it were, my conscience would come first. SENATOR SISTER PEGGY BUTTS

I think there has been a change in the perception of what's right and wrong. Wrong now is what you get caught at. WILLARD "BUD" ESTEY, FORMER SUPREME COURT JUSTICE

There's no right or wrong. There's only truthful or untruthful. ROBERT DUVALL, ACTOR

⌇⌇

When you work in the public eye and live out loud, each sentence uttered is a potential landmine. A passing reference to race or gender can be—if not career-limiting—at least credibility-threatening. Even a simple slip of the tongue can be costly.

I've told the story a thousand times, but it bears repeating because the lesson I learned was an important one. Words matter. Early on in my days as co-host of *Canada AM*, a G-7 economic summit was being held in Canada. We had a stellar list of guests coming up on the program, and so at eight in the morning I announced—live to the nation—that we would have interviews with Pierre Trudeau, Margaret Thatcher and the then chancellor of West Germany, a man I proceeded to introduce as "Helmut Shit"! I was mortified, fearing I had not only jettisoned my own career but also likely set off an international diplomatic incident. My boss, Bruce Phillips, assured me there would be no international crisis, nor would I be summarily fired or dispatched to some far-flung journalistic gulag to do penance. But he then said something that changed my life and still echoes in my head every single day of my working life. "Pam," he explained, "people won't believe you said that on TV." As I made my way up Parliament Hill to carry on with my day's work, sure enough, half a dozen strangers came up and said they thought they had heard me say "shit" but that they must have misheard! In a split second, the import of Bruce's comment hit. The power to speak the truth with which we are entrusted—by the viewers—is a heavy burden. Ever since that incident, I've been very conscious of my choice and use of words because words *do* matter.

I have found that when you speak directly and honestly and without any kind of bullshit, most people react without any kind of anger.

SAUL RUBINEK, ACTOR

Actors and friends Tom Jackson and Graham Greene appeared together on the program and on several occasions referred to each other as "big Indians." "Indian" was a word we had used as kids, and I didn't know if it was back in vogue. When I asked if I could use that word, they said, kindly but firmly, no. Who gets to say what is first and foremost a matter of intent. This issue came up in my conversation with writers Richard and Sandra Gwyn:

Sandra has a very good sense of humour, but she is a passionate Newfoundlander ... She's normally quiet and shy, but if anybody in her presence tells a Newfie joke, she will kill them.

Sandra nodded her agreement:

I get very fired up in defence of my people. Newfoundlanders have always hated that word Newfie. It is considered very derogatory. And when it becomes attached to jokes, it's just too much ... It's a matter of dignity.

In order not to offend, we must be careful about our choice of words, but it's also true that political correctness has silenced many, making people afraid to say or do what they mean. Joni Mitchell was an exception. She sat chain-smoking throughout our interview, and when I asked her if she wanted to offer the viewers a disclaimer, she turned to the camera and said: "For all children watching this, don't ever do it. For all adults, mind your own business." Then she smiled, having made her point.

The late Mordecai Richler was known for his sharp wit and biting commentary. His refusal to succumb to the forces of political correctness cost him dearly in some circles. But he continued to speak the truth in his writings and through his fictional characters. We had a wonderful conversation about all of this at the time of the publication of his Giller Prize–winning novel *Barney's Version*:

> The character Barney is someone outraged or offended by all kinds of dogmas—whether they come from the left or the right—or by special pleading of any kind. And I guess so am I.

~~

> Comedy, in terms of the human species, is definitely a survival tool because it's a way that we learn to face the truth. It's the only palatable form of truth that we can take. And whenever someone says something true, we just laugh and that's really interesting. ERIC IDLE, COMEDIAN

> Basically we tell the truth. We don't make stuff up. We start with the facts. The politicians give us the set-up—we just create the punchline. RICK MERCER, POLITICAL SATIRIST

~~

Humour is needed more now than ever. We must poke fun at ourselves … I think we take ourselves awfully seriously now.
CHRISTOPHER PLUMMER, ACTOR

Once on *Coach's Corner*, sportscaster Ron McLean read a list of nouns and adjectives that hockey icon and self-declared loudmouth Don Cherry had been called over the years. The list included moron, pinhead, blathermouth, bully, vain, crude, troglodyte, butcher and misogynist. Don confessed he didn't know what a misogynist is, but when I asked him how he feels when people call him a redneck, his quick retort was predictable:

> I love it. When the Scottish and Irish and English came over here, they were bent over working construction, working hard, ten hours a day. Because they were bent over, the sun burned their necks, so that's "redneck." So when you call a person a redneck, it's someone who works hard—I love it. Thank you.

Don knows that his unstoppable need to live out loud, both loudly and provocatively, might well have consequences:

> I expect to get fired from the CBC. There's no question. They'll say, "Don, we're going in a new direction" (isn't that what they say, Pam?). "Hey," I'll say, "I had a good ride, I'm ready to go. I've been on a long time. I had a good ride. Toodle-oo."

We identify, we empathize with one another to the degree that we laugh at everything that we have in common.

<small>LILY TOMLIN, COMEDIAN</small>

Chapter Eleven

Putting a Little Love in Your Life

I am absolutely convinced that what makes life really rich,
what increases spirit, has to do with love.
DR. SHERWIN NULAND, AUTHOR

Sherwin Nuland, best-selling author of *How We Live* and *How We Die*, has spent a lifetime dealing with those facing their final moments, and from them he has gleaned a powerful insight into the role that love plays in our lives:

> It has to do with our ability to express to those relatively few people who are important to any one of us what their lives mean to our lives, what our lives can mean to them. We're so bad at letting people know how we value them. That's the great moral change that I would like to see happen ... the very unself-conscious expression of what one's life can mean to others.

Dr. Nuland's comment, of course, applies in many circumstances because love takes many forms. We have intimate relationships, working partnerships, passionate friendships, and attachments to pets—even inanimate objects—that can create a powerful bond. I recall reading a wonderful line about relationships—the more traditional kind—which suggested that a good marriage is one in which each appoints the other the guardian of his solitude. Few couples I know have forged that rare bond.

The formidable duo of Richard and Sandra Gwyn agreed to share with viewers the secret of their successful marriage: "We laughed at the same things." To have watched Richard and Sandra together is to understand a partnership. They were friends, they were the first readers of each other's work, they did indeed laugh at the same things and, as he nursed Sandra through a long and fatal illness, Richard made every moment count. He read to her and discussed the day's news with her, and they continued to entertain friends—the salon simply moved from the living room to Sandra's bedroom.

When I spoke with Pierce Brosnan, he explained that he too had lost his soulmate to cancer. "We were a brilliant partnership and it was a two-way street," he said. His quiet charm and stunning 007 good looks had us all swooning in the green room, but he captured my heart when he described his late wife, the actress Cassandra Harris, as "the needle in my compass." The late Mordecai Richler often spoke of his wife Florence as a partner in the writing process: "Florence is the first person to read anything I've written and she's also the editor I count on more than anyone else."

Emmylou Harris has a voice that can make you feel her pain, and the lyrics she writes are shot full of it. She lost the love of her life, Gram Parsons, a gifted musician who died when he was just twenty-seven. She spoke about the pain in the lyrics of the songs she writes or records:

> Most of the songs we are drawn to are about pain because life
> is hard and there's no getting around it, there are no shortcuts.
> Just grab the nettle and jump right in. The songs that make us
> feel better are the songs that shine the spotlight on that. It's
> cathartic.

She went on to become the reluctant Queen of Country, but never
forgot her loss:

> I don't think anything gets easier. I think you get stronger.
> There's always something in your toolbox to fix whatever you
> have to deal with. I'm probably still a romantic, although a
> cynical one.

Other luckier souls find a love that lasts a lifetime. Hume
Cronyn made his acting debut in 1931. He and actress Jessica Tandy
were married for fifty-three years. Needless to say, I couldn't resist
quizzing him on the secret to such longevity:

> We had great mutual respect. She was more talented than I
> was. She had real magic. I had some skill, but she was magic.

Carl Reiner said Estelle, his wife, holds the secret to their marriage,
one that has lasted sixty years:

*It's almost impossible to
have a relationship and it's
very isolating. I'm probably
as lonely as anybody else on
the planet.*
kd lang, SINGER AND
SONGWRITER

185

My wife says, "Marry someone who can stand you." And that's it, isn't it? That goes for the long run. It's easy for love and lust, and that can go on for a long time. And the liking has to be there too. And then you see the little errors, the little flaws in people, and if you can stand that, everything else falls into place.

Thomas Moore has been a guest in the studio several times over the years. In one conversation, we focused on true love and whether mere mortals can experience it. "Matters of the heart are very important to the life of the soul," he said, and then continued:

> When you're with somebody who seems to have so much depth or so much humanity that you just love being with them, I think what you are sensing is their soul … In fact, heart is both a safe harbour for the soul and the route to it. A lot of experiences that we have in our life … open up the heart so that we allow the soul out. Usually we keep the soul life down, we keep it repressed because we just can't handle it. And, at certain moments in life, like when you fall in love perhaps, suddenly your reason gets dimmed and your soul takes over.

I found myself nodding vigorously at the whole idea of falling in love as a "dimming of reason." We've all fallen head over heels in love or fallen, knowingly and passionately, for absolutely the wrong person.

Despite the outcome there are seldom regrets, because of the seductive power of feeling something so close to your core, even if it is short-lived. Perhaps that's why I was so taken by my conversation with Nicholas Shakespeare, writer and descendant of the Bard, who had recently experienced love at first sight:

> You've got to be brave when you feel that. You've got to carpe diem—seize the day. You mustn't do it too often. But I think there are some things—actually you're powerless to prevent what you feel and I think it becomes a question of whether you allow yourself to take the next step. What's the point in being alive if you're not courageous?

One of the first feminist powerhouses to emerge from the sixties was Germaine Greer. She was almost blushing as she confessed that she had recently fallen for the wrong guy, at least an unlikely one. A handyman had come by to fix a problem, and there was an immediate attraction. "Is this it?" I asked. "Is he the one?" She smiled, shrugged and replied, "I am an expert in the fear of commitment."

Despite the fear of commitment, the risks and the consequences, most of the people I talk with believe in romantic love. In fact, I recall a great conversation with hugely popular Irish novelist Maeve Binchy, who for years kept a separate residence from her partner, writer Gordon Snell. Eventually, for the sake of cost and convenience, they moved closer, and finally into a duplex—together, but separate and apart. Maeve laughed at her own peculiar behaviour, but was firmly

I may be smart and can sit and do crossword puzzles all day, but, certainly in matters of the heart, I am not very wise.

STEPHEN FRY, WRITER
AND ACTOR

convinced that distance, however contrived, was one of the secrets of the success of their relationship. With two authors living under one roof, the need for personal and private space is easy to understand. Life might well become creatively complicated. Binchy described their rules of engagement:

> We both sit at a long table, cats curled up, and work from seven until half past one or two; then we read to each other what we've done in the morning. If you don't like it, we have a rule that you have to be completely honest and truthful. Once, Gordon said to me when I was writing *Glass Lake*, "I think that character is going to make me throw up, she's so goody-two-shoes!" Sometimes I've had to say about one of his verses that I don't think it's funny, which can be very hurtful.

So, I asked Binchy, how did they deal with the hurt?

> We have this strict rule called "Sulking Time." If you get a criticism, then you're allowed to go off and sulk for ten minutes. But then you have to come back and say either "I think you have a point" or "I think your criticism's wrong and it's going to stay as it is," but you're not allowed to go and nurse the grudge.

Timothy Findley and his partner, Bill Whitehead, who have been together for more than forty years, say stick-to-it-iveness is also the secret to their relationship. Findley explained how they keep it together:

> In a relationship you must say, "Goddammit, this is not going to do us in ... we're going to weather this and grow through it and find new aspects of ourselves and use this bad time as a way of gaining more maturity and a new hold on what it means to be alive." And, once you've started doing that, you think, "God, what if we hadn't? What would we have missed?" We wouldn't be nearly as capable of survival as we are now if we'd just shrugged and said, "Oh, well." Too many people shrug it off.

I am always intrigued by these conversations. But close working relationships are just as intimate and fragile as any romance, and there are lessons in each world applicable to the other. Isn't this exactly what we mean when we say "my other half"? Music legend Art Garfunkel talked about his other half:

> I ran into Paul Simon when I was eleven and I thought, here is another kid in the neighbourhood who is funny and different and understands. We both laughed a lot, we had a similar sense of humour. You need someone who understands you. Otherwise, you're not sure if you're filled with wonderful stuff or if you're just different.

Michael Budman and Don Green—The Roots Boys, as they are known—are co-founders of one of the most successful brands in the world. And they too have rules to make their partnership work, as Michael explained:

> We're both flexible, and one rule is that if one person really believes more than the other person in a certain idea or principle, then we'll go with that gut feeling. We give.

Roberta Bondar has her own unique approach to relationships, both professional and personal:

> If you have a vision and you find that someone doesn't share the vision, you either change the vision or change the people you share it with.

The nature of my work is such that not only are the hours long, they often don't jive with those who have a more traditional Monday-to-Friday kind of schedule, which is, of course, most of the rest of the world. It means relationships are difficult to start and even more difficult to nurture. Searching for clues to how others have coped or adapted, I frequently query those with similar dilemmas, including the diva of domesticity herself, Martha Stewart. She is a powerful lady and has a reputation for setting the rules and playing on her terms. I was warned not to ask her about her personal life, but when the question came up rather naturally in our conversation, I simply probed a little by asking what was missing from her apparently perfect life. She surprised me and the audience with this frank answer:

> Well, I'd like to get married again. I miss the everyday contact with a single person, and I think that would be very nice to have once again.

Her dream man?

> Someone who is a little quirky, a little unusual, self-sufficient, someone amusing, intelligent, who'll put up with me.

Martha knows, all too well, that her success and celebrity are intimidating for mere mortals. If you work on television, everyone assumes that you have countless options and suitors at every stage door. Not so, says the voice of experience. Now, there's no doubt I am a happier person when I'm in love, but I'm not unhappy when I'm not. In a partnerless world, I simply spend more time with friends and work a little more because, through my work, I find real satisfaction and company that I enjoy. And though I had never heard it put this way, I loved the description offered by octogenarian Doris McCarthy, who declared herself "happily unmarried":

> I have never been married and I have had a thoroughly fulfilled life. There's no room in life for everything life offers—not in any one life.

A person who is loved always has a stronger sense of well-being. A person who does not know they are loved can never be happy, they can't.
GEORGE CHUVALO, FORMER BOXER

On more than one occasion, I have listened to men talk with passion and desire about the objects of their affection and relationships that would surely qualify as love. BB King calls all his guitars "Lucille," and while he confessed that, if forced to choose, he would take flesh and blood over wood and strings, it's a close call. And Pinchas Zukerman loves his ladies too:

> I met her—my fiddle—in 1963. She is about 250 years old. She's from Italy. She eats spaghetti. I am really nice to her. Because if I am not nice to her, she is not nice to me. It's an attachment. She is never out of my sight.

Authors also often talk affectionately about their creations—their labours of love—or about giving birth to their books or nurturing them through adolescence into adulthood. Here's how Ann-Marie MacDonald described the relationship:

> I spent five years on this book, and when I write something it's like my child and, of course, I love it. And I want it to be a precious gift that I will give to the reader. I want the reader to feel like nobody wrote it, that it's their own. Because that's how I feel about my favourite books. I have an intimate relationship with them. And God knows, I don't *want* to meet the author, so why anybody wants to meet the author is beyond me. It's going to wreck it.

It sounds so corny—what you need to sustain yourself through life is love.
GEORGE CHUVALO,
FORMER BOXER

One of the most extraordinary conversations about love and relationships and communication was sparked by an innocent question about frozen food. With just a mention of "hockey puck food," as he calls it, Graham Kerr, formerly known as the Galloping Gourmet, waxed eloquent on the importance of preparing food for loved ones and gathering around the table to share it with them:

I understand the lack of time. However, if that takes over completely, then there is almost nothing that you do originally as a way of expressing how much you love them, and even if that is hard to do, the person who is on the receiving end feels so loved and so cared for and so special that to drop it as a means of communication … it's survival, it's restoration. I've increased as a person because of it, and I'd hate to see that go. The dinner table is really the last tribal gathering place. I think people gather around the television and think they're having a relationship—you know, yelling "Hey, get me a coffee" during the commercial breaks—but that's really not a relationship. A relationship is like having a non-skid tire on your car … with studs and everything else. We have non-skid tires on our personas—we don't want to skid—and you have to get those off to expose the inner tube of our life, which is not an easy thing for people to do. And it has to come gradually, and I think you get massaged into that at the dinner table.

Life is a smorgasbord.

kd lang, SINGER AND SONGWRITER

Nana Mouskouri is one of the most famous recording stars in the world, with 450 recordings and CDs, 250 honours and awards, and several other positions, including serving as a Goodwill Ambassador for UNICEF and as a member of the European Parliament. In answer to what motivates her, she said, "All you need is love." In fact, half of the songs she sings have the word "love" in them:

> I was a war child, and I needed to express myself and I was always trying to find love, trying to find peace, trying to find hope through my songs. I think we cannot live without love. It's so important. We all search for love. Everything we do is love. The world is troubled, and we have to return to love.

ᔦᔨ

Many of the people I meet offer wise words on love and relationships, but there are occasional moments of brilliance. Often the most profound insight is deceptively wrapped in the simplest phrase. Tom and Melissa Gallant's story is one of courage, devotion and the triumph of the human spirit. It's also a story about the "middle of love."

Tom Gallant is a musician, a songwriter, an acclaimed playwright and a sailor. He's articulate, warm and funny. His wife, Melissa, was a lively, bright, athletic, independent woman who ran her own restaurant. Both shared a love of the sea and led artistic and adventurous lives. In July 1992, as they made their way home from work one night, their van was hit by a bus. "In a split second, just like that, everything changes," Tom explained. Melissa suffered what the experts call a catastrophic injury. For weeks she was in a coma, on life support with drains in her head. When Tom recovered enough to visit, Melissa's heart rate doubled at the sound of his voice. But he quietly told her not to come out of the coma just yet because she needed time to heal before her body could cope with the strain of consciousness.

Day after day, even when the doctors said there was no evidence of recovery from the brain injuries, Tom made the pilgrimage to her bedside. "When you see your beloved in that kind of trouble, you are given the love to do the job," he explained. The neurosurgeon said there was little hope of recovery, and they were advised that the best option was permanent institutionalization for Melissa. But Tom said no, believing that "there was still wisdom in there." Then Tom went on to explain to me the real lesson he had learned was about the "middle of love":

> You find out what love really is ... You see, we're all fascinated with the beginning of love—we write movies and songs and books about it, or we talk about the end of it, you know, we write books about divorce. But we don't spend any time on the middle of love. And the middle is you have to be willing to sacrifice for your beloved. Before you think of yourself. In sickness and in health. Period. If it had been me driving, she'd have been there for me.

There were days when Melissa begged Tom to leave her, to start again and make things happen for himself. Tom didn't buy it:

Any time she's telling me to leave, she's trying to be kind. As terrible as this has been, there are joys in it that are just as deep. You sit and watch somebody get devastated like that and watch her rebuild herself using humour. We made a miracle together.

Breaking with the Pack

I remember the moment I figured it out. And I recommend this to people:
Ask yourself questions. You may get an interesting answer. And I asked
myself out loud, "What ground do I stand on that nobody else stands on?"

CARL REINER, COMEDIAN AND WRITER

F inding that new ground can be risky, not to mention lonely. Breaking with the pack does take courage and confidence. Perhaps "chutzpah" is the better word. In the fifties, Reiner, who has a dozen Emmys, wrote and produced (with Mel Brooks) Sid Caesar's classic *Your Show of Shows* variety program. But the newly emerging TV audience was demanding to see their lives— or perhaps the lives they were searching for—reflected on the screen. The situation comedy was born. There were no models, so Reiner wrote of what he knew, turning to his own family life as the inspiration for the groundbreaking *Dick Van Dyke Show*.

Many creative people must take risks and do something no one else has done. The audience doesn't want to keep reading the same book or hearing the same tune, and the artist never knows how the readers or listeners or critics will react. Even the award-winning, internationally successful Margaret Atwood feels pressures, and she shared with me her sense of them:

> Think of it—what could be more risky than going in with nothing but what's inside your head and what you can do with your hands? You have nothing else. You don't have a forest to chop down or something you dig up out of the ground or a company or any of those sorts of things. You have what's in your head and what can come out by your hands, and that's it.

E.L. Doctorow put it this way:

> Writing a book isn't a matter of putting sentences down on paper. It's a matter of expending yourself, or risking yourself, because when you finish a book, you're completely different.

When you're standing there on that piece of ground that you've staked out and you're all alone, you often begin to question your own judgement. Why am I the only one here while the pack is over there? In life, it's so much easier to run with the pack and be part of the gang. We learn very early on that being different often means being ostracized or punished. It is one of my greatest concerns about the world of journalism. Pack journalism is what you see on campaign planes or on Parliament Hill—the reporters have the same clip and basically tell the same story at the end of the day. If not, their editors will ask, "Why are you saying this? That's not what the competitor has said."

Breaking with the pack and having the courage of your convictions—and challenging others to do the same—has a cost, but it's usually worth it. As Farley Mowat said, "I've been known to stick my neck out pretty far, but I've never had it chopped off."

❧

I thought I would much rather invent things and start things and create my own world and my own reality than to go down a very well-travelled highway. ROBERT LANTOS, FILMMAKER

There are people everywhere telling you what to do. Distrust authority. Distrust other people telling you what to do. You've got your own gut feeling. We're all so different. MICHAEL PALIN, ACTOR, COMEDIAN AND WRITER

I look back and I'm proud and in a sense I am awestruck by what I have been able to accomplish. I had to overcome resistance from the state, from the church, from the public on occasion—only occasionally—but I also had to overcome my own inner fears and anxieties and stress, and that's what I'm proudest of. DR. HENRY MORGENTALER, HOLOCAUST SURVIVOR AND PRO-CHOICE CRUSADER

❧

Breaking with the pack is not about believing you're better or special. It's not about ego. It's about trusting your own instincts and your own talents. A young man named Ben, who was married and had three young children, was working at an insurance company and holding down a second job moving furniture to help make ends meet. But inside him was a driving desire to sing. He decided to take voice lessons on the side. They worked. Ben Heppner is now one of the most sought-after tenors in the world. He talked about the decision that resulted in such pleasure for all of us:

> I decided I had to do one thing. I gave myself a limited time to see if I could accomplish this. I didn't know how this would turn out. I had no idea I would end up in this. It still befuddles me.

His success befuddles no one else. His voice is extraordinary. Ben remains as humble as ever despite his international stardom, and I am not surprised. When he was first a guest on the program, not only did the power of his voice make my body vibrate and my heart wrench, but then he presented me with a rose. It was a lovely gesture. Usually, it's the performer for whom the flowers are tossed respectfully on stage. But I should add that Ben is not a total risk-taker. As he told me the next time we met, on his way home that night, he stopped to buy a bouquet for his wife, just in case she'd been watching TV and had witnessed how his charm had cast its spell.

We often tend to think of risk-takers as adventurers like Richard Branson, who set his sights—and a vast amount of cash—on flying around the world in a hot-air balloon, or like others such as astronaut

I'm very comfortable working without a net. I just give myself over to a project and trust that whatever is going to happen is going to happen.

EMMYLOU HARRIS, SINGER

If you want to try something, you should try it and do it, and either it will work or it won't, and you'll be the better for having tried it.

SHIRLEY DOUGLAS, ACTOR AND HEALTH CARE ACTIVIST

Colonel Chris Hadfield, whose adventures in space are unrivalled. As he explained, often those who break new ground meet resistance:

> It has always been difficult to convince the status quo that exploration is worthwhile. The Lewis and Clark expedition was not universally popular. The first people to cross the Atlantic were not universally recognized as having done something significant in history. But the long-term, historic impact … of those explorations has been tremendous, and we don't do this because everybody thinks it's a good idea. We do this because enough people think it's a good idea that we can get it done.

Hadfield told me that he'd always wanted to be an astronaut but was reticent to confess his heart's desire. From his youthful vantage point, it didn't seem likely that a small-town boy could become the superman of another century:

> We all put limits on ourselves by saying, "I can't do that." But very few things are done by people who aren't trying to do something new.

The night that he joined us in the studio, there were other guests and crew clamouring for his autograph. "The sky is not the limit" is how he signs the much sought-after photos.

What I like about Paul Quarrington's view of life is his sense of adventure and his sense of humour. On his official resumé he declares,

I always felt I had a destiny that was different. I wanted to be a spaceman. We didn't have these wonderful words—like "astronaut"—then.
ROBERTA BONDAR,
ASTRONAUT

"Every year there is a quantum leap in my ability to skate backwards." When I quizzed him about the relevance of this seemingly useless bit of information, he smiled and confessed that while he still can't skate backwards, he is practising. Usually, however, Paul's adventures take him much farther afield than the local hockey rink. When we last spoke, he had just written about a trip he took with his father and daughter to the Galapagos Islands, the site of much of Charles Darwin's early research. Quarrington said that he had gone in search of signs of God in Darwin's theory and ended up learning about parenthood, perseverance and taking risks:

> Darwin was fearless. He realized that his theory was going to cause some great concern and undermine the way society was working at that point ... not just notions of religion, notions of a god ...but really the way everyone assumed that things were set up was challenged by him. But despite that, he went ahead in the service of knowledge ... fearless exploration in the fields of knowledge.

Retired Major Dee Brasseur was one of the first women in Canada to graduate as a pilot in the Canadian Armed Forces and became one of only two female CF-18 fighter pilots in the world. "You've got to find something you love doing and do it for a living," she advised. It also took courage and a willingness to risk a job she loved to come forward with her story of sexual abuse in the military. "It was heaven and hell," she told me. But she found her voice and,

I have always felt that there is a tremendous amount of entertainment value in going somewhere you wouldn't go normally—a world that's outside your experience.

ATOM EGOYAN, DIRECTOR

I became what I could be.

NANA MOUSKOURI, SINGER

in doing so, forced the military to begin to clean up its act. As the story of her life implies, she's not one to do things halfway:

> If you're not living on the edge, you're taking up too much space. There's only one way to go—all out.

Gordon Pinsent has been performing for more than five decades. He has a favourite quote on his fridge: "Leap and the net will be there." Professionally, he says he wishes he could find roles that would allow him to take more risks, roles that would take him to the edge:

When asked to do things, say yes. That's the important thing.
DORIS McCARTHY, ARTIST

> Just leap, because it's going to mean you are extending your possibilities from a standpoint of unlived experiences. I love the stuff that arrives on Monday and you get to do it on Tuesday. And if it happens to be outrageous, then on Tuesday you have to do something quite outrageous.

It's learning the rules and then breaking them.
CAROL SHIELDS, AUTHOR

Emmylou Harris said she feels she owes it to her audience to take risks but acknowledges that people are more willing to let you do that once you have achieved some measure of success. She explained her thoughts about risk:

> The thing about risk for me is that I feel that from the very beginning what I did was different, and I got successful enough at it that I thought that was supposed to be my job. I almost would feel I were letting my constituency down if I

didn't, so I'm supposed to take risks, and when an opportunity comes your way for something that you know is intriguing or at least interesting, whether or not it's successful commercially or even artistically, you should do it.

When Jann Arden was just starting out, it was hard for her to find her confidence. She lost faith in her own talent, put pressure on herself and tried to second-guess people's expectations of her:

> I worked myself into a froth and got into a corner and kind of panicked and was writing the most ridiculous things, and I went to my manager's house and played him a few things and he said, "Well, even your really bad songs aren't that terrible." So I thought, I'm going to stick to the three bloody chords that I know and I'm going to do those and I'm not going to try and be something that I'm not. I had to live up to one of my own credos, which is Be Yourself at All Times, and I just sort of lost sight of that.

❦

> You've just gotta keep believing in yourself and, no matter what the fashion is, you gotta say, "Well, there's room for everybody. They have to take me the way I am or we don't do it." TONY BENNETT, SINGER

I am male. I am masculine, so when I'm sensitive, I still have that masculine touch. Why would I ever change? When they say that artistry has to have a feminine touch, they're wrong. It's definitely wrong. Society makes it difficult for a male to express ... himself. But it's self-esteem and how strong a person you are that makes a difference. ELVIS STOJKO, ATHLETE

One thing I don't like is that you have to look a certain way to fit a mould. I didn't understand that, to be a country singer you have to wear a hat and wear boots and a big belt buckle. They all told me I needed to, and I said, well, I'm not gonna—so tough. VINCE GILL, COUNTRY MUSIC STAR

ↂ

Isabella Rossellini, the beautiful actress and model, was let go from her assignment as the face of Lancôme. The makeup company was selling beauty, and in our culture that means youth, and Isabella was aging. She was sanguine about the decision, in part because she has always resisted attempts to perfect her imperfections:

We waste so much of our life comparing ourselves to something that isn't real. LINDA EVANS, ACTRESS

I didn't want to fix my chipped tooth. It's mine. Underline your individuality. Revere your imperfection.

When superstar Shania Twain was on the program, I could see first-hand her natural beauty. I was shocked—although secretly maybe a little relieved—to discover that even nature's beauties struggle with their own perceived flaws. Shania confessed what she dislikes about her body, which explains why she wears pants:

I don't like my legs and I've got to get out of this. I'm going to force myself. I'm trying to get more comfortable with my body—I'm just like everybody else.

The White Rose of Athens, Nana Mouskouri, has remained—even in an age of fleeting fame and one-season wonders—a superstar of epic proportions. And she did it all while wearing her trademark horn-rimmed glasses!

This is my complex. The little fat girl with the glasses. I had to accept myself. I was hiding behind them, and I thought that if I could give something, if I could do something right, then the glasses wouldn't bother me. I don't like concessions in life in order to succeed. I think if you have something to say, people will listen to you. If you don't, they won't listen because you look beautiful. And this may be one of the reasons the audiences like me. People tell me that, without the glasses, I wouldn't be Nana any more.

Chapter Thirteen

Embracing Change

My vision of age had been entirely confined to defiance ... I'm going to go right on doing everything I did before ... take that! ... And it wasn't until I was about fifty-five that I realized that doing everything you did before was not progress.

GLORIA STEINEM, FEMINIST AND AUTHOR

Gloria Steinem and I talked at great length about her enthusiastic embrace of the most inevitable of changes—aging. She describes her post-sixty years as a "new country" and declared, almost gleefully, that "the older I get, the more intensely I feel about the world around me." So I couldn't resist asking if she had any regrets or missions left unaccomplished. She shot back—with a smile on her face—"There are a lot of things I regret: mostly being too nice." I think that we all feel that way from time to time. Gloria was not, however, talking about being kind or nice to friends and strangers, but rather about being tougher on the powers that be in terms of demanding change and calling people on their bad behaviour. And what she discovered is that a few grey hairs and the odd wrinkle had given her the freedom to do just that:

By the time I was sixty, I realized, "Hey, there's this whole new period of life here that nobody told me about that is as free—more free—than what I felt when I was seven or eight or nine or ten or eleven or before the feminine role came down and started to control us and the central years of life.

Gloria made an interesting point about character, saying that other than becoming a little wiser with age, we are pretty much who we've always been:

> The best indicator of who you are going to be after sixty is who you were at nine or ten, except now you have your own apartment and you're hopefully smarter.

At eighty-something and still painting masterpieces, Doris McCarthy should know. "I think as you age you get more like you are," Doris told me. When I posed the predictable question about how, at eighty-six, she viewed her circumstances, Doris went on to explain:

> I predate feminism … There isn't any aging issue. You get older. And it's wonderful. At forty I thought, thank God, that's all over. I'm free—I have my life in my own hands, and from then on it got better and better and better. I have news for you people. It gets better.

Doris says every decade has been better than the decade before because she has finally learned to live in the moment:

Being this age is wonderful because you've dropped your fears. You can enjoy every day for its own sake. The fact that you don't know how long you're going to go on and it's getting more and more limited means you appreciate what you have. It's a great time of life. I embrace life just as much today as I ever did. In fact, I think I embrace it more because I have learned to enjoy it right now—what I am doing now—and not think how nice it will be when I get home.

~

I remember when I turned fifty and I had a dinner party and I was very careful to only invite people who were older than I was, and we sat around the table and talked about it and not one of us was willing to go back. Everyone felt very comfortable where they were. CAROL SHIELDS, AUTHOR

I think about what kind of old lady I will be. I'm going to go lame eventually. I've got a collection of canes ready and I'm going to poke people with them. JONI MITCHELL, SINGER, SONGWRITER AND ARTIST

I've had a fantastic run. Nothing can last forever. So anything now is a bonus.
PHIL COLLINS, SINGER AND MUSICIAN

~

Men don't talk as much—or as willingly—about the process of aging. Fortunately, there are exceptions to every rule, though it seems aging is just less of an issue for men, particularly in terms of sex appeal and career. Pierce Brosnan, a sex symbol on screen, has a great perspective on the changes aging brings:

I think I'm at a point now where I'm hungry to explore, take more risks, make a difference, to grow. You have to keep the energy and innocence alive inside yourself—not get brittle.

ᢒᢙ

It's easier when you're older. About the only good thing about all this grey hair is that you are a little more believable to all these young punks. MARIO BERNARDI, CONDUCTOR

What you see is what you get. You hope that with some degree of experience and age, I am more understanding, more compassionate and patient. JOE MANTEGNA, ACTOR

As you get older, you try to stop fooling yourself and be as honest as possible about what you are, who you are. PHIL COLLINS, SINGER

ᢒᢙ

Solitude is not found navigating the Web. That is isolation. Not solitude. The same is true of television. An hour or so is fine. All day is a problem.
UMBERTO ECO,
PHILOSOPHER AND AUTHOR

The philosophers and the poets have long pondered the question of whether age brings wisdom. T.S. Eliot wrote that the more we know, the less wise we become because wisdom often gets lost in the onslaught of information and the accumulation of knowledge. Others beseech us to remember that kindness is more important than wisdom, noting that once you figure this out, you are becoming wise. I think it was the late great journalist I.F. Stone who once observed that "when you are younger you get blamed for crimes you never committed, and when you get older, you begin to get credit for virtues you never possessed. It evens out." During our conversation, Allan Fotheringham offered his take with declarative simplicity:

> Age gives you wisdom, and when you get there you'll find this out.

Linda Evans is the actress and beauty queen who played Crystal Carrington on the soap opera *Dynasty*. But as the years ticked by, the opportunities diminished, and Linda left Hollywood behind to become a women's health advocate. I thought a discussion about Hollywood's cult of youth could prove interesting, if she was up for it. Well, she was. And she had some thoughtful advice on embracing change:

> After every door closes in your life, there's an opportunity to see yourself differently. People come into our lives and leave, so take what you got from them, then go out to see what's next in life.

And women, she said, must start to learn to like themselves and the changes that are inevitable:

> I really feel like it's important for women at some point to go inward. If we're going to live ninety years, you can't do it and

God, please give me the vision to see when it's over and give me the grace to step down.

GARTH BROOKS,
COUNTRY SINGER

You start realizing that you've said hello at least as many times as you've said goodbye.

JANN ARDEN, SINGER
AND SONGWRITER

look outward all the time, it doesn't work, because it is an inward journey after about forty-five—whether you like it or not. You're not going to be comfortable unless you go in and find something about yourself that you really like and respect, so that you can take yourself through the rest of this time when the rest of the world is saying, the best is to be young. I like myself so much better now than when I was twenty or thirty.

This was a message my guests repeated time and again. If you are not comfortable in your own skin, dealing with myriad forms of change—as individuals and as a society—will be most disconcerting, perhaps debilitating. Fortunately, with age generally comes a greater confidence, and we are much less vulnerable to the expectations of others.

"Happy" is a much overrated word. There's something called serenity and just this place of contentment, and I'd much rather be there.

JANN ARDEN, SINGER AND SONGWRITER

❧

I feel I can step down from my pulpit now and join the congregation and hope there is a vat of sacramental wine. FARLEY MOWAT, AUTHOR

Part of the enjoyment of growing old is not to think about it too much—just to enjoy what comes to you and relish the experiences that you have. PATTI PAGE, SINGER

I don't care what people think of me any more, and I am free. That's one thing about getting old—it does give you the freedom to be who you are and to speak your truth and to be you. DR. MARION WOODMAN, PSYCHOTHERAPIST

The older I get, the more I realize "who's perfect?" Let's not cast that first stone. And there are two, four, twelve sides to each story. Things are not always what they appear to be. JOE MANTEGNA, ACTOR

༄

Although aging may mean freedom from fear and from the judgements of others, it does not diminish the desire to have left our mark in some small way.

I think I want to leave a little bit of some value. If I can move the frontier a little, I'll be happy. I'll never know if I did or not, though, thank goodness. SENATOR LAURIER LAPIERRE

I think the essential thing is to leave. Leave the stage with a little bit of love. And hope that you have amused people and given them some pleasure during your time. That's the main thing. SIR GEORGE MARTIN, MUSIC PRODUCER

I don't think my children are interested in my legacy. That's gone and past. All they remember of my time in politics is that it was a bloody bore because daddy was working hard. But that doesn't mean they are not going to take an interest

in the future of our country. Pierre Elliott Trudeau,
former prime minister

~~~

Carol Shields is an amazing storyteller, and for her, aging, like plot, unfolds inevitably:

> I'm interested in the arc of the human life … It's the only plot that really interests me, and there's no going back in time, it's an aging process, it's life going on its way towards death, and that seems to me just about the only thing really interesting to write about.

There is always the fear that we will get too set in our ways and lose the passion and drive to meet new people and tackle new ideas. Doris McCarthy had a solution:

> I still take a course at the university almost every year—just for the joy of learning something and of being with young people. They are great to be around. They live a life I could hardly imagine in my day. Their lives are, in many ways, mysterious to me. But my life is mysterious to them. They have no idea in the world what fun it is to be my age.

Neil Peart talked to me about the importance of keeping an open mind as time marches on:

I'm not a cynic, I'm a skeptic. I won't put things down before I understand them, but I'm a skeptic in that I won't embrace them before I understand them, either.

∽

While aging is the most inevitable of the changes we must embrace, we also live in the real world, which is increasingly ruled by technology. As we attempt to navigate through the most powerful period of change in human history, we're not exactly sure where we're headed. Darwin reminds us that it is not the strongest of the species nor the most intelligent that survives—it is the one that is the most adaptable to change. We will all be put to the test. Thomas Homer-Dixon has named our dilemma:

> The most predictable thing about the future is that it is completely unpredictable. Things happen that we won't expect and we won't have anticipated—I call this the problem of "unknown unknowns."

Circumstances change. What you want in a politician, in a political leader is a person who is capable of adapting to a circumstance. And the circumstances vary.
SENATOR LAURIER LaPIERRE

Even science fiction—one of the ways we often used to look into the future—is having a hard time, because the pace of real change is now far outstripping the science fiction writers' ability to conceive fantasy. William Gibson, the man who invented the term "cyberspace," says he has "no idea" what's really going to happen, other than the obvious fact that computers will soon be gone because we will all be wired directly:

Earth is the alien planet for me. I feel like I'm using science fiction as a huge set of oven mitts to get a grip on the red-hot present.

Getting a grip on the present is no small task. I found this in my own life, because as a journalist I was a chronicler of all this radical change, but as a survivor of change I didn't have a clue. Being fired at forty, with no savings and a substantial mortgage, does make "coping with change" a personal mission. As the old saying goes, "There's nothing like a hanging at dawn to help focus the mind." I smiled, although sadly, when I heard the phrase used in quite another context. I had the opportunity of attending a small private dinner for Archbishop Desmond Tutu, former chair of the Truth and Reconciliation Commission on apartheid-era crimes. He is one of those men who, despite his diminutive stature, commands a room and your undivided attention when he speaks. Of his battle with cancer he said, "When you have a potentially terminal disease, it concentrates the mind wonderfully. It gives a new intensity to life." I knew what he meant, although obviously not in that life-or-death way.

We are all reluctant recruits to the world of uncertainty. Yet an enforced change is sometimes just the incentive we need to reinvent ourselves or head off in another direction. Either it can create opportunity and inspire a new intensity about your mission or it can be paralyzing. Singer Loreena McKennitt expressed her fear this way: "My concern is that our lives are being so crowded out by all that change and complex technology, that we have so little time to sink our roots into real experiences that engage our souls."

I'm disappointed in the hysteria that always attends change.
WYNTON MARSALIS,
JAZZ MUSICIAN

The promise of technology was that it would reduce the amount of time it takes to do any one task, but it also seems to lead to an exponential increase in the number of tasks that people are expected to do. The computer is becoming ubiquitous. Personal relationships suffer because everything we say and do must, for the sake of time, be abbreviated or fragmented. Handwritten letters have all but disappeared, e-mails have been stripped of nuance—not to mention grammar—we place those annoying little happy faces at the end of the e-mail to express our emotion, and a brief voice mail or a few personal words scrawled across the top of the fax cover page substitute for keeping in touch.

The phrase "information overload" doesn't even come close to describing the endless amount of information we are bombarded with and the relentless pace at which it comes at us. It intimidates, overwhelms, and sometimes we feel guilty because there is so much more to know and we can't find the hours in a day or a week to consume it all, never mind process it, according to Umberto Eco:

> This is one of the great problems of our time. We were
> fighting all millennia for increased information and now we
> are killed by an excess of information. You become an illiterate
> because you're paralyzed. Any person—not just scholars—
> today must retain a hundred times the amount of information
> in his or her own brain than a person at the time of the
> Romans ... but can you say that Plato or Aristotle were less
> intellectual than we are?

This dramatic change is not only altering personal relations and the ways we interact, but also redefining work, intelligence, culture, and, most profoundly, changing our expectations. In other words, change is changing our basic social contract, the implicit bargain between citizens and between citizen and community. And in response we—predictable human beings—try to impose some order on the chaos, as Booker Prize–winning author A.S. Byatt explained during our conversation:

> We are an animal that loves order, that loves complexity, that needs frameworks.

Martha Stewart, a control freak after my own heart, made a similar point:

> If I had to choose between beauty and function, I think it would have to be function. Things have to work. I have a tremendous amount of flexibility. I just have to plan for my flexibility.

But that will be easier said than done, as author Ann-Marie MacDonald explained:

> Something is going to get lost and something is going to be found. Something new is going to get born. And you're going to lose things you can't bear to lose and you're going to find things that you never expected to find.

Chapter Fourteen

Learning from Experience

We learn from the past. If we know the past,
we know what to do in the future.

Tony Bennett shared wonderful stories of his early days and a circle of friends that defined music in the last century. Before our conversation was over, each of us had proposed marriage to the other. We didn't follow up, but let me state the obvious: it's hard to resist the charms of the man who crooned a million tunes and left his heart in San Francisco. He was first named Best Male Vocalist in 1951, and more than fifty years later he's still a hot commodity. "If you love what you're doing, you'll never work a day in your life," he said with a broad grin. But he owes both his longevity and his success, he says, to a lesson learned in childhood. When Tony was still a boy, his father died, leaving his young widow to raise the family. Tony's mother, a seamstress, began to take in sewing. She always took pride in her work. "But once a day she'd get angry, throw a dress over her shoulder and say, 'Don't make me work on a bad dress, I only want to work on the good ones,'" Tony explained, "so I've never compromised, I've kept my integrity and I will only do quality songs." Ironically, the title of his most famous one—"Rags to Riches"—could be the story of his life. There may have been some bad choices or advice along the way that steered him off course, but not often and not for long. Tony Bennett used every experience wisely. "You learn from failure," he said, "you don't learn from success."

It is the most obvious of life's lessons. A misstep, a poor judgement call or simply failing at something that matters to you usually leaves you a little wiser. You then pick yourself up and start over. Failure is certainly not the only prerequisite to success, but it is a good teacher. And while failure can be devastating, it can also be a turning point—a catalyst for change—or a moment of revelation. As Deepak Chopra explained it, "Experience is not what happens to you, but how you deal with what happens to you."

If you are a ranking member of the Royal Family, then what happens to you and how you deal with it can set off an international scandal. Photos of the Duchess of York topless, having her toes sucked and caressed by a man who was not the Duke of York, were on every front page. A friend of mine had known Sarah Ferguson for several years and was asked to try to help her recover and reinvent herself as a non-Royal. But no one was sure whether Sarah had learned a hard lesson, and whether she would be able—or even allowed—to pick herself up and start again. "I've made mistakes and now I'm taking responsibility for my actions. I'm not asking you to like me," she told me when we met in 1996, just after the publication of her memoir, *My Story*. She

As I age, I know my range changes, but there is always music to be sung.

MAUREEN FORRESTER,
OPERA SINGER

Peace comes from within, and if you get that, then I think we're getting somewhere.

SARAH FERGUSON, DUCHESS
OF YORK

went on to describe the first step in the process of moving forward:

I think if you look through the Bible, you'll see that forgiveness is very important. But it's not just "I'm sorry." You've got to really feel it in your heart and suffer and go through the pain of the mistakes you've made. The Lou Gehrig's Disease [amyotrophic lateral sclerosis, or ALS] conference was a month after the photos, and I was crawling with such humiliation and embarrassment. Crawling. I didn't want to go to the conference. I've been with this organization for seven years, but I tried to get out of it because I had nothing to give them …
I felt I would disgrace them, so I didn't want to go. But they wouldn't let me get out of it, and when I arrived at the conference, I was shaking. And I got out of the car and I met Kevin Langdon from Australia, who had flown all that way over. He was unable to walk. He was in a wheelchair. And he said, "Look, I'm going to get out of this wheelchair and I'm going to walk and if I can blanketyblank walk, then you can hold your head up high and you can walk into that conference room because you haven't got a disease, you've got good health, and you get in there and you support us. Smarten up. Okay, so you've made a mistake, but we want you here." And when I walked into that room—three hundred people—many with ALS—they stood up—a lot of them with the help of their caregivers. Well, I lost it, because they were my friends and they were dying, yet they stood up for me. They were saying

I had been there for them and they were also there for me. I have never ever forgotten that day. By being there with them—some of them can't even hug their own children—I realized just how lucky I am.

Judy Blume has written twenty-two books for teens, and if there's just one message she hopes they hear, it's this:

It's okay to make mistakes, and if you learn from your mistakes, that's really good, and don't beat yourself up for all of your mistakes. Apologize once and get on with it.

Author and actor Ann-Marie MacDonald, in both her fiction and in her life, has come to a firm conclusion on this:

Redemption is about confronting the truth, making it whole, embracing the contradictions or the ugly things or the unspeakable things, and saying, "This too is part of who we are."

British actor, author and comedian Stephen Fry is blunt, animated and disarmingly honest. He told me the story of how he walked off the stage one night—in the middle of the run of a play in London—and simply disappeared. His career was in jeopardy. He called it his "wobbly" time:

I just suddenly felt, "I don't know what I'm doing here." I felt as if I'd been on a highway in the fast lane and suddenly realized that, though I was in a very nice car and going incredibly fast, I had absolutely no idea where I was going. I had a crisis. But crisis—as you know—is the Greek word for turning point. It's not necessarily a catastrophe or a calamity. But it can have catastrophic circumstances.

Well, it was a turning point. He survived the crisis and recommitted to his career. Fry's work has afforded him the luxury of what he calls the bohemian life—a student enrolled in the school of life. The goal of such education is self-knowledge, which is, after all, learning from your experience. Fry had much to say about this:

> I knew what I wanted to do, I just didn't know what I wanted to be, which is more important. Oscar Wilde said that those who know what they want to be from an early age—a successful grocer or a politician or a judge—invariably become it, and that is their punishment. If you choose a mask, then you have to wear it. But for those who live an "artistic" life—or the eternal student life—for them, it's different. They never know where they are going and they cannot know, because their only goal in life is self-knowledge, and that means they have no idea where they are going to be in two years' time—I have no idea where I'll be in two years' time.

I finally realized it's easier to go forward than it is to go backward.

Jann Arden, singer
and songwriter

Diane Dupuy was called a slow learner by the experts and a "retard" by the kids in the schoolyard. What she did have was a vivid imagination. "It was my mother who recognized that I had a very special talent—my imagination—and she encouraged me to use it," Diane explained. After repeated attempts to pass high school, she finally took a job as a cleaning lady at an amateur theatre so she could save money to buy puppets and become a puppeteer—a logical result of a childhood she'd had to fill with imaginary friends. She created the now internationally known Famous People Players—a black-light theatre troop whose performances feature the mentally challenged members and their puppets—and has succeeded against all odds. A wiser Diane Dupuy knows why:

> Everybody learns from everybody's mistakes. Failing is really wonderful—it's really good to fall on your butt, because you really learn so much from all your mistakes. Famous People Players has been one mistake after another, and that's what helps us grow. We cry a lot on the road—we get on the bus and we deal with it. And I learn more.

But never underestimate a little sulking time. Often the initial response to a failure—real or perceived—is anger. The trick is to allow yourself time to hurt and feel sorry for yourself and time to grieve for what you've lost. It's a necessary step. But stop short of wallowing in the anger.

Frank McCourt had a lifetime of things to be angry about, but he also offered a warning when we spoke:

If you are bitter or if you are angry, it limits your ability to look at things. Anger is a kind of weakness because you're leaving yourself open. Humour is powerful.

～

Anger is very important. Anger is like an energy cell. But we have to be able to take our anger and do something positive with it. GLORIA STEINEM, FEMINIST AND AUTHOR

Mutating anger into comedy into laughter is a very good way of transmuting anger into a useful thing. It turns both anger and sadness into positive uses of energy. ERIC IDLE, COMEDIAN

My mother says, "When you get angry, that's good for you. If you hold it in, it makes you sick."
DIANA KRALL, SINGER

～

As we age, said Idle, we actually do—fortunately—change our minds:

When you are young, you have this complete moral view of what's good and what's bad and who's good and who's wrong, and when you get older, you find that you meet all the people you thought were wrong and they turn out to be rather nice people. And you think, "Why did I hate them? They were lovely, really." I think that sort of savage anger is about youth.

Actor and director Saul Rubinek has a very successful career, but in Hollywood one bad movie can derail a future. Saul looks at these so-called failures in quite another way:

I was probably in the most reviled movie of the last fifty years—*Bonfire of the Vanities*. There was a movie that didn't work. None of us really knew that it didn't work. But did I have fun doing that movie? I had a blast. The terrible movies were the most fun.

And what did he learn?

All you can do is go with your own instinct. I can't make movies for other people. I go with what I think is honest and has humour and has meaning. And if it's at the right time and the right place, God bless it. If it's not, what can you do? If you try somehow to manipulate your life in order to please those people that might help you, you're screwed.

As we all know in this business, longevity requires talent.

JOE MANTEGNA, ACTOR

Frank McKenna is a politician who dared to change his mind and sometimes paid the price. He ruled as premier of New Brunswick for a decade and learned some powerful lessons from his experience at the helm:

Sometimes you can have all the facts but you come to the wrong conclusion. That's when you've got to decide if this is the bridge you want to die on or whether you need to beat a strategic retreat.

Now, speaking of beating a strategic retreat in the face of defeat, the stories that make me wince with sympathetic pain often come from writers who spend months, sometimes years, of their life putting their soul on the line, only to realize—their own call—that it's not good enough. E.L. Doctorow learned that lesson the hard way:

> If anything resists you when you're writing, you must stop, because it's wrong … You have to know when to stop and when to reassess what you're doing. I wrote 150 pages of this book and they were so boring, it was awful. And I thought, if I could write this badly about something so innately dramatic, I have no business being a writer. And I threw the pages across the room and sat down at the typewriter and started to type something else.

Others, like Maeve Binchy, found their voice when they turned to what they knew:

> My first few attempts at writing were rejected. So I started writing about what I knew about, and I write as I spoke, which made me believable. I always set my books in small towns because it's easier. It's a good explanation of why everybody meets everybody—otherwise, how would I organize the characters to meet? All my heroines were born when I was born—in 1940—so I don't have to do a spot of research!

Anne Michaels says failure goes with the turf:

> I think that a writer has to have a very intimate relationship with failure, because failure is almost inevitable.

Writing is like driving at night in the fog. You can only see as far as your headlights, but you can make the whole trip that way.

E.L. DOCTOROW, AUTHOR

Mistakes are not failures of character or ability, they are often just another way of doing things. And if it's true that we learn from failure, then one might also conclude that never having failed means never having achieved or learned. Sir Richard Branson has achieved much, in part, he says, because of lessons learned from failure—and life:

> Life is so rich and full of so many challenges. On the one hand, I say to myself, you know, you only live once, you've got to push life to its limits, you've got to see what you're capable of and go for it. On the other hand, one shouldn't really take risks when you're a father and you've got children, and strangely, as I've gotten older, I've gotten quite a bit more sensible.

As for regrets, I guess we all have a few. As Branson said, if we'd known then what we know now, we might have been more confident in our own judgements—or even made different ones. But more often than not we regret that we didn't speak up or speak more loudly. Few of the many successful people I've talked with really regret much about the choices they've made.

෨෬

> We all have a past and we're all trying to live with it one way or another. BRUCE COCKBURN, SINGER AND SONGWRITER

I can't regret stuff that I've done. What's the point of regretting? It's energy wasted. kd lang, SINGER AND SONGWRITER

I don't think anyone can live a life without doing things they are ashamed of, but I wouldn't want to change anything else. AL PURDY, POET

⤳

There are a few regrets in BB King's life. He wishes he'd finished high school and that he'd owned up to some parental responsibilities earlier in life. When he was about six, his father abandoned the family. A few years later his mother, whom he adored, ran off to live with another man and BB was taken in by relatives. But his mother died young, and soon afterward he moved back into the sharecropper's cabin on the plantation where he and his mother had lived. At age ten he was living on his own, milking cows, working in the fields and sometimes as a houseboy for the plantation owner. He got his first guitar at twelve, and the rest is history. He turned into not only an extraordinarily talented blues musician but also a man who very much believes in taking responsibility for yourself and your actions.

He arrived in the studio on the day he was being presented with yet another gold record. He was wearing a starched white shirt, a tie, a giant gold ring and a constant smile. Wonderfully charming, he was very forthcoming about his own reputation as a lover of the ladies. He had, over the years, fathered fifteen children with fifteen different women! Some he married, some he didn't.

> Each time I got married I thought this was going to be the one time. Like the children, I didn't plan this—and that's the terrible part—I should have planned.

Despite the regrets, BB learned from his experiences. He neither denies nor shirks his paternal responsibilities. There are no secret, guilty handouts, nor are there any blood tests. For each who asks, there is a helping hand. But no cash and no free lunch, just a fat cheque to an institution of higher learning in his child's name. You might quarrel with the womanizing and lack of planning, but never with his willingness to pay for the consequences. Instead of blaming a lousy childhood and a frenetic career, BB King faced the music and made amends.

One of the sources to which I so often turn for inspiration and guidance is the writing of Sydney J. Harris, an American journalist and author who wrote a syndicated column, "Strictly Personal," for more than forty years. He died in 1986, and I never had the opportunity to either meet or interview him. Among the many brilliant insights that are his legacy is a rule I have come to live my life by: Regret for the things we did can be tempered by time. It is regret for the things we did not do that is inconsolable.

I recall a story that my friend the late Al Waxman, an icon of Canadian culture, told me when he was last on the program:

When I was a kid—about twelve—I went down to what was then called Maple Leaf Stadium to see the Toronto Maple Leafs Triple "A" ball team play. Jackie Robinson was playing second base for the Montreal Royals, and I didn't know about race or colour—I was too young to have been educated with any biases. All I knew was that I was looking at an incredibly gifted ball player. He gave me one of the most exciting afternoons I have ever had, just watching that man play baseball. Years later, when I was going to acting school in New York, I got on a plane and there was Jackie Robinson—bent over, looking old and tired and grey. And I thought to myself, "He doesn't want to be bothered." But I wanted to go over to him and say, "You gave me one of the great afternoons of my life and I just wanted to shake your hand and say thank you." But I never did—I was too chicken. So what if he would have said, "Don't bother me"—which I know he wouldn't have said. He would've said, "Thank you." But I didn't go over to him, and a week later the man died. And I thought to myself, never, ever again will I not take the opportunity if it presents itself to go over to someone and thank them and tell them how much I enjoyed their work.

I take nothing for granted, which can make for an interesting life.

WILLIAM GIBSON, AUTHOR

Al always did that. Often, when I'd get home late at night after the program, tired and worried about tomorrow, I'd find the message light blinking and there would be Al's voice with a kind word of support, saying how much he'd enjoyed the show and the guest or my laugh. Not many people in a business dominated by egos would take the time or make the effort, but he had learned from his experience.

Finding Your
Own Measure

⊷⌣

I never really wanted to be a businessman,
I just wanted to achieve something.
SIR RICHARD BRANSON, ENTREPRENEUR

Sir Richard Branson—by now it's obvious how impressed I was with him each time we talked—calls himself an "adventure capitalist" and is, by any measure, a successful businessman. His British-based Virgin empire is one of the world's best-known brands. With some two hundred companies, nine billion dollars in annual sales and more than forty thousand employees worldwide, the Virgin label is attached to everything from records to airlines, from bridal gowns to life insurance.

When British pollsters pose questions on life after the monarchy, Branson's name always crops up as a potential president. One poll named him most suitable to rewrite the Ten Commandments, second only to the late Mother Teresa. So when the "hippie entrepreneur" was in our TV studios, I asked him what, in the world of business, would be his first commandment. His answer says a lot about the man:

> Loving thy neighbour, looking for the best in people and just generally being decent with people is probably the most important thing.

His philosophy is to enable others to achieve what he's achieved. If one of his companies grows to more than a hundred employees, he starts a new one so that people can still rise in the ranks, take some ownership and develop a sense of loyalty. Branson wants people to find satisfaction, and not just financial reward, in their work. Here's his secret to success:

> A little bit of creative bullshitting sometimes is appropriate. But generally, the way to be successful is to find good people and look after them. Motivate them and make sure that they believe in what they are doing, because it's important to be the best in whatever field you get into. Your company is only as good as its people. If you have a tremendous bunch of people working together, all pulling together, you can achieve anything.

As I promised in my opening notes, the people whose words grace the pages of this book have achieved, accomplished and succeeded. But, first and foremost, they are successful human beings, and that, in many cases, has helped to make them successful in the more traditional sense of famous or financially secure. Most have a mission in life and are passionate about it. And all have a strong sense of purpose. They want their acts and actions to matter, to count. What I have learned through my many encounters with these extraordinary individuals is a different way of looking at this thing called success and its counterpart, achievement. If achievement is about doing the best you can, then success is just the praise from others for what you would have done anyway. By that measure, achievement is far more satisfying. Success is just a bonus. And so we each find our own measure— to define our success or explain it. And it's seldom about awards, as the composer Marvin Hamlisch, who has won three Oscars, four Grammys, three Emmys, a Tony, three Golden Globes and a Pulitzer for songs such as "The Way We Were" and the Broadway musical *The Goodbye Girl*, explained:

> If you came to my apartment, you would not see the Oscar. The truth is, it's really not about that. It's really about wanting to do what you can do as well as you can do it for as long as you can do it ... Yeah, the penny dropped when I got my three Oscars, but you know how long the penny drops for? You have a great evening, you've got all these people around you, you come home and you've got these three Oscars—which, by the way, you have to give back so they can put your name on them, which, by the way, you pay for—and then the next day, it's basically business as usual, you get the twenty calls of congratulation and on you go.

⌇⌁

I don't think what I do is about awards. It's a nice compliment, but it isn't any more than that. In terms of being creative and doing what's there to be done, it has very little to do with it. BRUCE COCKBURN, SINGER AND SONGWRITER

I think, as you grow older, particularly if you are successful, it becomes less important because you realize how transient it is, how temporary and how hollow. I'm not kicking it, I'm very grateful for it, but it's not the most important thing in life. DORIS MCCARTHY, ARTIST

The award is: Are people liking the book and do they want to give it to their best friend? That's the award. ANN-MARIE MACDONALD, AUTHOR AND ACTOR

⌒◠⌒

Finding our own measure is often a reflection of the work we do and the contribution we make. I've always seen journalism as more mission than profession, a mission to inform minds and incite a civic sense. For those of us in search of work that matters, there was one powerful example for me. In the 1970s, two young journalists—Bob Woodward and Carl Bernstein—cracked the Watergate cover-up and wrestled a president to his knees and out of office. So years later, when I had the opportunity to interview Carl Bernstein, I bounded into the green room (a waiting room for the guests that is never painted green) to confess the influence he had on me and my enthusiasm for his work.

"Could we start with a little perspective on Watergate a quarter-century later?" I asked, promising that there would be plenty of time to discuss his new book in the course of the hour. He shot me a nasty look—and through what I swear was a curled lip, he barked, "Save all this for the studio, will ya," and turned away. At that moment I thought, if ever I lose my sense of mission or begin to feel so resentful about the trappings of my job, I hope someone takes pity and drags me off the scene.

᠆᠊

Here now is how many "successful" people have taken their own measure:

> You can have a good book that isn't "successful" and doesn't make a lot of money, you can have a bad book that isn't successful and doesn't make any money, you can have a good book that is successful and makes a lot of money, and you can have a bad book that is successful and makes a lot of money. There is no correlation between literary goodness and success and money. All you can do as a writer is try and respect the page. Try and respect the reader. Try and respect who is going to pick up that page. That page is all you have, that is your sole means of communication, so try and make that page as good as you can make it for where it is in the book. That's all you can do. MARGARET ATWOOD, AUTHOR

The secret of my success? Going through life is never about winning or losing or being "successful" or making lots of money. It's not about that. It's about challenging yourself and being able to juggle things that come at you, because the only thing we can control is our reaction to the things around us, and we don't have control of the things that happen around us. ELVIS STOJKO, ATHLETE

If I ask myself at the end of the day, "What is true meaning?" am I going to measure it by the fact that I am able to walk around? I don't think so. It was the most amazing experience and opportunity from so many dimensions. I learned so much about myself, about other people, and it's so gratifying to be able to give back. I have given a lot—but I've been able to receive so much. RICK HANSEN, ACTIVIST

I don't rate things by good, better, best in terms of my work. In other words, I put everything I have into that project I am doing at that moment and it has all my attention, and anything I did in the past is the past and the future hasn't happened yet, so I can't worry about it. JOE MANTEGNA, ACTOR

I'm doing my best. I am happy. I try to stay interested. I try to find drama in life. I try to take responsibility for my actions and I try to act sympathetic to the people I care for. Looking at it in terms of success or not success is less interesting to me. RICHARD FORD, AUTHOR

The great gift is to have some way of thinking you may have made a little difference in the world. GLORIA STEINEM, FEMINIST AND AUTHOR

Being needed and useful is the biggest recompense you can have in life. ISAAC STERN, VIOLIN VIRTUOSO

Epilogue

T his collection offers just a sampling of the countless wonderful exchanges I have had and of what goes on in the minds of those I've had the pleasure of spending time with over the years. And what I have tried to do is give you a sense of the common themes that emerged from so many of the conversations.

But the things that are most difficult to recount in the pages of a book such as this are not the ideas, but rather the nuances of the face-to-face encounter—the smiles, the off-camera remarks, the genuineness or lack thereof—those brief windows into a person's soul. Often it's just a split second that offers the real insight into someone's character, and too often the cameras miss those moments, too. So from my vantage point in the studio, I may have a very different sense of the person than you, as a viewer, do. And of course, as viewers, we all bring our own biases to the television set. Let me just say that, from where I sit, what has endeared so many of these people to me is a sharp wit and a self-effacing sense of humour. These are difficult attributes to capture on the printed page because they're all about timing and context, yet as Eric Idle so shrewdly pointed out, we all use humour to keep things in perspective. Comedy, he says, is a survival tool because it helps us face the truth. Or as Dame Edna so succinctly put it, comedy is a huge "massage parlour" for the human spirit.

Although there is more pain than comic relief in her lyrics, Emmylou Harris agrees that facing the truth and being honest is the key to life: "When you're shooting straight for the heart of the matter, there's always a chance you're going to overshoot or make a fool of yourself. When you're going to come right to the edge with your emotions, you can get overly sentimental, but the best thing to do is to simply state the truth."

Easier said than done. It is hard enough to be honest with others, harder still to be truly honest with ourselves, about ourselves. But in the darkest hours, just before dawn or when you catch your own reflection in the mirror or when the stage lights have dimmed and those who are paid to praise have fallen silent, it's almost impossible not to see through the first few layers of a protective persona.

Part of what I do in the course of my work is to try to strip away some of these layers so that you can see a character revealed—in the sense of being able to see a person's true core and the stuff they are made of. You see, often because of their chosen professions, the people I meet and talk with live in a bubble or cocoon created by money or fame. Those who believe their own reviews—who think they are the icon they have become for the public—are often those without a moral compass and therefore they don't know where to turn or how to act because they lack "a moral framework" to guide their behaviour. They don't have much of value to add to any conversation.

But those who survive this rarefied experience—with humanity, integrity and life intact—do so because they know themselves. They are self-aware. They live examined lives. Ironically, stage actress Martha Henry says acting has taught her about stripping away layers to get to the truth of an emotion. Acting, she explains, is not so much about assuming a character as it is about revealing one—your own. It's the same for most of us in our chosen professions: we are successful only when we are prepared to be honest and to open ourselves up to others, even if it means we're a little vulnerable.

That's why the people whose words were chosen for this collection have become successful human beings—because they were able to risk revealing themselves to themselves and to us.

Still, the successful know their limits. Scientist Stephen Jay Gould reminded me of the great words of the British writer G.K. Chesterton, who, roughly paraphrased, stated that the most important part of any painting is its frame: that is, the essence of art is limitation. Gould's point was that we should recognize there are boundaries to what we can do in life too. I know I am unlikely to ever become an astronaut or an Olympic skater. I know my limits. So it's not about backing away from challenges; rather it's about putting your time and energy into what matters most and into efforts where you can truly make a difference.

If there is no naïveté in those who have become successful human beings, there is little cynicism in them either. Lily Tomlin made the point by quoting one of her famous characters, who always says: "No matter how cynical you become, it's never enough to keep up." And I think Allan Fotheringham spoke for many when he said that he and others are not cynical, they are simply "bruised idealists."

Experience may have taught many of my guests some harsh lessons—they may have slipped back before moving forward—but all have emerged with a much stronger sense of self. Elvis Stojko concluded that life was not about winning or losing or being "successful" or making lots of money: "It's about challenging yourself," he explained, "and being able to juggle the things that come at you, because the only thing we can control is our reaction to the things around us." And that's exactly what the wise ones do. As Frank Shuster said of his work with partner Johnny Wayne: "Our secret was knowing what we could do well." The gentle and eloquent country singer Vince Gill expressed it this way: "I worked hard to make this gift work—but the gift was given. And I think sometimes people have a tendency to think they're special when they've been given a gift; they forget that what's special is the gift, not the person."

The most enjoyable part of my job is always the chance to challenge the guest to a little lateral thinking, a concept discussed earlier in this book. I always relish the opportunity to ask the scientist about rock music or the politician about favourite fiction writers, and vice versa. The answers are always surprising and show the character through yet another prism. We and they are seldom simply what titles or gender or age suggest. We are all eclectic in our interests, and we are never the same person all the time. All of us, regardless of whether fame and fortune have smiled upon us, do have the opportunity, as Germaine Greer said, of waking up most mornings and reinventing ourselves: "I do all kinds of things and this is still me." Or, as the talented young singer Kim Stockwood said: "The bottom line is that you have to be who you are." And that can be many things. Circumstances can call up out of us behaviour or actions that even we didn't know we were capable of.

Clearly, the most powerful force that unites the wonderfully wise whose words you have read in the preceding pages is their attitude. Call it what you will—mind over matter, the glass is half full. It's infectious. "I regard every milestone along life's road as a challenge and a great opportunity," declared Dame Edna. Songwriter Randy Newman put it this way: "I think I'm not an optimist. But I try and think optimism is the way to go. If you're optimistic, even when bad things happen, you've at least had a couple of weeks of looking forward to it."

Artist Mary Pratt also inadvertently offered a clever bit of insight on the importance of keeping things in perspective during a conversation about how the artist works: "It's just paint on a board. You have to be brazen enough to think that. If you make a mistake and you don't know it's just paint on a board, you can feel that it's your life at stake. It's not." So many times in our lives we believe that we or the work we do is indispensable to the future of the world—that our presence is required in order for success to be ensured. But we too must accept the fact that we're just paint on a board—that there is always more paint and there are many other boards. As we often say in TV when a technical problem occurs and a crisis ensues, just remember this isn't brain surgery; it's just TV, no lives are at risk.

Along with the humour and a refreshing honesty, there was also guidance from many of my guests on facing the future. In essence, what they all shared was the view that if we have lived with dignity throughout our lives, then that—and only that—is what will bring dignity to our final days. There's no cramming for this final. Astronaut Roberta Bondar was most eloquent: "I think I'd be afraid of dying if I thought that I had unresolved issues or tasks that had not been fulfilled." So live in the moment and try to leave the world a better place than you found it. As Jean Vanier said: "The whole of the mystery is that every person has a mission. They have a life to be lived." He also stressed the importance of our relationships and the need for a sense of commitment and fidelity. Vanier's words are very broadly defined, however. There are relationships with loved ones, but also with those who cross our path in the course of everyday life. You can't listen to those people, he noted, unless you slow down long enough to give them your attention. It's worth doing, because if we listen, we are changed.

I couldn't agree more. We do learn as we listen to others, and that's what this book has been about—listening and then acting, not just with our heads but with our hearts. What's most significant in life is that which is invisible to the eye, not the material things we so often crave.

I fear that all this may sound just a little pretentious. It's unintended. But just in case, I shall give the last word to a man who is anything but pretentious. Paraphrasing Helen Keller's statement that no one can consent to creep when one feels an impulse to soar, Don Cherry declared in our conversation that, "It's tough to soar like an eagle when you're mixed up with turkeys."

I can only hope you've enjoyed your flight with the eagles.

Index